SOLID GOLD

TRAINING THE GOLD'S GYM WAY

BILL REYNOLDS, PETER GRYMKOWSKI,
EDWARD CONNORS, AND TIM KIMBER

CONTEMPORARY
BOOKS, INC.
CHICAGO

Library of Congress Cataloging in Publication Data
Main entry under title:

Solid gold.

   Bibliography: p.
   Includes index.
   1. Bodybuilding.   I. Reynolds, Bill.
GV546.5.S65   1985   646.7'5   85-13310
ISBN 0-8092-5189-2

All exercises photographed by John Balik at Gold's Gym, Venice, California.

Models: Tim and Chris Glass, Lori Innes, Roger Laubscher, Marya Curry, Hal Butler, Julie Stangl, Ellen Morrow, Vickie Schiff, Cindy Lee, Tim Belknap, Ann Slater, Janaire O'Hara, Dawn Marie Gnaegi, Charles Glass, Tom Platz, and Maria Gonzalez.

Black and white photos printed by Isgo Lepejian, Burbank, California.

Published by Contemporary Books, Inc.
180 North Michigan Avenue, Chicago, Illinois 60601
Manufactured in the United States of America
Library of Congress Catalog Card Number: 85-13310
International Standard Book Number: 0-8092-5189-2

Published simultaneously in Canada by Beaverbooks, Ltd.
195 Allstate Parkway, Valleywood Business Park
Markham, Ontario L3R 4T8 Canada

CONTENTS

FOREWORD

Bodybuilding is an exacting process, and it's possible for a man or woman new to the activity to stray away from correct training methods. And at the beginning and intermediate levels of bodybuilding, this can be disastrous. Faulty and possibly dangerous workout habits can follow you for a lifetime of pumping iron.

With the instruction and advice presented in *Solid Gold*, you won't develop unproductive training habits. The authors are all recognized bodybuilding experts. Pete Grymkowski won the IFBB Mr. World title and has co-owned Gold's Gym with his partners, Ed Connors and Tim Kimber, since the late 1970s. And Bill Reynolds, the Editor-In-Chief of *Muscle & Fitness* magazine since 1978, has authored more than 30 books and 1,500 articles on all phases of bodybuilding.

I consider it an honor to have been chosen to author the Foreword to *Solid Gold*. It's the type of book I wish had been available when I began serious, systematic bodybuilding training. I would have saved a lot of time blundering down blind alleys of training information if I'd first read *Solid Gold*. And if you are new to bodybuilding, you'll be able to avoid my own early mistakes after you've read the book.

Tim Belknap.

Solid Gold is the first beginning- and intermediate-level training book that includes exercises and routines for both free weights and Nautilus, Universal, and other machine-oriented training. So you can use this book to master the training rules, exercise performance, and workouts you need to muscle up, regardless of where you train. This is probably the greatest strength of *Solid Gold*.

As long as you follow the advice presented in this book and train consistently, you'll make great progress toward achieving the powerful physique you've always wanted. So, throw on your training gear and get into the gym for a heavy session of pumping iron. Train the proven Gold's Gym way using *Solid Gold* as your guidebook. Good luck with your workouts!

TIM BELKNAP
Mr. America, Mr. World,
Mr. Universe

*The joy on **Albert Beckles'** face says it all.*

1
THE BODYBUILDING LIFESTYLE

To borrow from Charles Dickens, bodybuilding can be the best of times and the worst of times. The best of times occur when you win a competition and are up on the stage receiving your well-deserved trophy. And the worst of times occur in the gym during a highly intense workout when you've been eating so little that your stomach thinks your throat has been cut.

Correctly applied, bodybuilding training with weights can literally change your life. We've seen the sport turn mice into lions, severely over- or underweight young men and women into persons with normal body weights, pencil neck geeks into champion athletes, and weak, sickly individuals into robustly healthy men and women. At Gold's Gym, miracles like this occur almost every day, so we must be forgiven for being a little blase about these miraculous changes. But they *do* happen with great frequency.

On the other hand, incorrectly applied bodybuilding techniques build very little muscle, nor do they significantly improve physical fitness. *And* incorrect exercise form can actually lead to physical injury. That's the main reason why we have taken such care to teach you only safe training techniques in *Solid Gold*, plus in its predecessors, *The Gold's Gym Book of Bodybuilding* and *The Gold's Gym Training Encyclopedia*.

Hundreds of thousands of men and women have trained the Gold's Gym way—either through our literature, or in an actual Gold's Gym—and virtually all of them have experienced remarkable results in building muscle and generally improving their physiques. You will receive the same superior physical progress as well, *if* you follow our instructions to the letter.

Solid Gold is intended for men and women with between zero weight training experience and about 6–8 months of steady workouts. So if you want to start packing on impressive muscle mass, you've come to the right place.

WHAT BODYBUILDING CAN DO FOR YOU

Without question, weight training is the most highly intense form of exercise known to man. And it changes the shape of your body faster than any other training method. Listen to **Rachel McLish** (twice Ms. Olympia): "Women waste thousands of hours in unproductive aerobics classes when only a few hours of weight training will yield equal results. So if your time is limited, why not use the type of exercise that yields the fastest and most dramatic results? Weight training."

In a purely physical sense, your body shape will change, your strength will dramatically increase, your energy levels will improve, your health will grow better, and you will gain an increased sense of self-worth with just three 30-minute bodybuilding sessions each week.

An average man over a six-week period can add a half inch to his upper arm measurement, and add comparable new muscle mass to his shoulders, back, chest, and legs, while reducing fatty body stores around his waist and hips. In only six weeks of steady training with weights, the man's strength levels will increase by 50%–100% in most exercise performed in a bodybuilding workout. By any standards, these are remarkable gains!

An average woman in six weeks will tone her arms and upper body while reducing fatty stores in her hips and thighs. Her strength levels won't increase quite as dramatically as men due to hormonal differences between the sexes.

But one of the biggest changes we've seen in novice bodybuilders is attitude. They gain great self-confidence and eagerly accept challenges which they would have habitually avoided prior to initiating a weight training lifestyle. Because they are now physically superior, they become more assertive, which in turn improves their entire lives. Who wouldn't want to make these changes in his or her life? With weights, you can!

THE PHYSIOLOGY OF MUSCLE GROWTH

Scientists use the term *hypertrophy* to indicate an increase in muscle mass, an augmentation of strength, and improved muscle tone. And hypertrophy is induced when you infrequently and briefly overload a muscle with resistance it is unaccustomed to handling. Obviously, hypertrophy is the object of heavy bodybuilding training.

Michael Neveux

Rachel McLish.

The *overload* you place on a working muscle group can take many forms. Most commonly you overload a skeletal muscle by forcing it to lift a poundage greater than it has ever lifted before. Similarly, you can overload a muscle by using a consistent weight in a workout, but do more reps with the poundage in strict form than you did in the past. Or you can overload a muscle by performing a consistent number of reps with set poundages, but complete the total program in less elapsed time than in a prior workout.

Regardless of how you overload a muscle group, the overload induces muscle hypertrophy. And as you progressively overload the muscle, workout after workout, you gradually accumulate a great deal of muscle mass. Of course, this is your goal as a bodybuilder, to build huge, well-defined muscles.

In Chapter 2 under the heading "Resistance Progression," you will find a complete explanation with several examples of how bodybuilders progressively overload each muscle group. And if you follow this procedure religiously enough, you will be rewarded by possessing a massive, symmetrical, well-proportioned, and super-muscular physique.

MEN VERSUS WOMEN

Anyone who glances at a handsome male bodybuilder or beautiful female bodybuilder can easily note some differences between the two sexes. But in this section we'll restrict our discussion to those structural and physiological differences that will affect competitive bodybuilding performance.

Because men secrete much more of the muscle-building male hormone *testosterone* than women, men will always be generally stronger than women. But relative strength levels are on parallel continuums, so it's possible for many naturally strong women to be more powerful than a naturally weak group of men. A good example of this is the phenomenal Australian bodybuilder-powerlifter Bev Francis who has bench pressed 330 pounds in competition, a poundage nearly twice her body weight. There are a lot of guys who weigh the same as Bev who would probably experience difficulty merely rolling that barbell across a lifting platform, let alone lying on their backs and pushing it from chest to straight arms' length!

An average male bodybuilder has what can be termed a balanced bone structure, without any overly large or small bones. On the other hand, women tend to have heavy leg bones and a lighter upper body skeletal structure. Therefore, taking into consideration a male and female bodybuilder with equal body weight, the woman could come close to holding her own in leg exercises, but she would be blitzed by the male bodybuilder in all of the torso and arm movements.

This might irritate a few of you overly macho types, but women have greater endurance and higher pain thresholds than men. For proof, just look at Olympic Marathon Champion Joan Benoit who defeats most of the trained male runners against whom she competes in open races. And in a percentage comparison of male and female track and field world records, Benoit's 2:22 is closer to the men's record than any other.

Both men and women secrete the male hormone *testosterone* and the female hormone *estrogen*, but men secrete primarily testosterone and women mainly estrogen. Testosterone makes men stronger and gives them leaner physiques with more relative muscle mass, while estrogen makes women less strong, allows them less muscle mass, and gives them proportionately greater body stores.

So, what's this have to do with bodybuilding? If nothing else, it tells a

woman that she'll gain muscle mass more slowly and to a lesser degree than men. But to compensate, her endurance and greater pain threshold allow her to take longer, more highly intense workouts that would virtually kill her male counterpart. Men, of course, are stronger, but they simply don't have the endurance to do a woman's lengthly, high-intensity workout.

Due to the unique physiological features of the two sexes, we're now seeing increasing numbers of male–female training partner units. The woman pushes for longer and more intense training sessions, while the man forces his partner to use heavier weights in her exercises. The net result is a better physique for each of the training partners. Give it a trial!

AGE FACTORS

As long as you have at least partial use of your limbs, you can benefit from pumping iron at any age. For a competitive aspirant the best years to start are in the late teens, but men and women have begun competitive programs in their 30s and still become champions. Simply put, younger bodybuilders make much faster gains of muscle mass than more mature men and women.

If you can maintain a child's attention span, you can get him or her to work out with weights as early as 8–9 years of age. And we've seen superfit senior citizens—both men and women—happily pumping iron in their 70s and 80s. So as long as a person is healthy, we recognize no age limits in weight training and bodybuilding. If you like pumping iron, do it!

THOSE INEVITABLE MYTHS

Despite the widespread public acceptance of weight training and bodybuilding, there are always geeks who'll tell you how ruinous the activity is. Following are the five most persistent myths with the truth behind each one.

1. *It stunts your height.* Lou Ferrigno is 6′5″ tall. And there are scientific studies that prove sports activity, including weight workouts, actually increases height.

2. *You'll get muscle-bound.* This contention was scientifically disproven in 1962. In reality, bodybuilders are much more flexible than the average person.

3. *You'll wreck your back.* As long as you follow correct training procedures, as outlined in this book, you'll strengthen your back rather than injure it.

4. *Women will end up looking like men.* You can disprove this contention for yourself by attending a women's bodybuilding show. They're foxes!

5. *It'll slow you down.* If it did, Olympic sprinting champion Valeri Borzov would never have lifted weights. Nor would have hundreds of thousands of other Eastern European athletes.

MEDICAL CONSIDERATIONS

Weight training is a much more intense form of exercise than you've ever tried before, so it's essential that you have a doctor's physical examination prior to commencing a training program in order to reveal any hidden, health-threatening physical maladies. Normally, heart irregularities crop up in middle-aged men and women, and they can be detected if you submit to a stress test EKG (electrocardiogram). If an irregularity is evident in the EKG, further tests will be ordered to pinpoint the problem, which can usually be controlled with medication. When on medication and under the supervision of your physician, you can usually follow a fairly brisk aerobic exercise program, perhaps even including some limited anaerobic work.

Younger athletes occasionally have hidden orthopedic problems which can be revealed during a comprehensive physical examination. For that matter, every man and woman embarking on a fitness program—and particularly one which stresses weight training—should take a physical exam. Once residual orthopedic problems have been identified, they can be worked around with a well-designed personalized bodybuilding program.

Tendinitis and other inflamations can be easily controlled with prescription anti-inflamatory drugs like Motrin and Feldene. One of our authors (Bill Reynolds) has an osteo-arthritis condition in his left knee from repeated trauma in college football games, and Feldene has worked quite well for him.

Weight training is an excellent method for working around injuries to maintain strength in unaffected areas. You'll always find exercises that don't cause pain in the injury site, and you should make good use of them.

DIFFERENT BODYBUILDING GOALS

There are seven clearly defined goals that can be pursued through weight training and bodybuilding methods, exercises, and routines. We will note all seven of the goals and include a brief justification of why you might decide to pursue this goal.

1. *Developing health and fitness.* Any type of physical exercise will help to promote buoyantly good health and superior physical fitness. But the great intensity of bodybuilding training—combined with the healthy diet initiated in the bodybuilding lifestyle—will promote fitness and health better than any other method.

2. *Bodyshaping.* Again, no form of exercise will change the form of your body more quickly than bodybuilding training, particularly when combined with a muscle-building diet. Of course, this is the reason why serious competitive bodybuilders train so hard with weights.

3. *Strength development.* You can do chin-ups and push-ups until you're blue in the face and still never develop a fraction of the physical strength resulting from heavy weight workouts. At a maximum, you can use no more than your bodyweight for calisthenics versus hundreds of pounds in many weight training exercises.

4. *Athletic conditioning.* Old-time athletes used to run for miles wearing heavy work boots, believing that this was the only means of getting into shape. Today's champion athletes would laugh at their predecessors. Today's athletes combine systematic weight training workouts, skill work in their events, speed-strength training, and a variety of other workout modes, all under close medical monitoring.

5. *Injury rehabilitation.* Regardless of the sport you practice and the level at which you play—from recreational slow pitch softball to intercollegiate football—training and participatory injuries are inevitable. Lost time retards sports results, so it's essential to immediately rehabilitate the injury, strengthen it to at least its previous level, and improve flexibility in the injured area, all in an effort to get a valuable athlete back into competition as quickly as possible.

Combining weight workouts with modern athletic training procedures has worked wonders in this regard. As long as the injury is to soft tissues, many athletes can be back competing at the highest level in only 2–3 weeks. And you can't beat that!

6. *Competitive weightlifting and powerlifting.* Weight training can be a sport in terms of weightlifting (which is a very popular sport in Europe and Asia) and powerlifting (more popular in America and Canada). In both weightlifting and powerlifting, athletes attempt to lift maximum weights overhead (Olympic lifting), or hoist enormous poundages in the squat, bench press, and deadlift (powerlifting).

All men (and many women) seem to wish to test their strength. If you do decide to test your own strength, you should first read Dr. Fred Hatfield's *Powerlifting: A Scientific Approach* (Contemporary, 1981). It's an excellent training manual, which can be found in all large book stores, or ordered at the stores if they have sold out.

7. *Competitive bodybuilding.* We've spent quite a bit of time in this chapter discussing the wide variety of activities in which barbells and dumbbells are used, but we haven't neglected the main thrust of the book, bodybuilding, which we define as the use of weight training workouts to change the body's shape. Serious bodybuilders, of course, compete in amateur and professional divisions both nationally and internationally.

Virtually every word in the remainder of this book is strictly bodybulding-oriented, and you'll learn everything you must know to get up onstage and win your first bodybuilding title.

2
GETTING STARTED RIGHT

Regardless of the type of resistance equipment you choose to use in your workouts—free weights or any of the many exercise machines found in larger gyms—there is a body of basic information common to the use of every bodybuilding apparatus. So you can master this vital information early in your bodybuilding career, we present it before any of the actual exercises and routines.

To add authenticity to this book, we have used actual quotes from elite male and female bodybuilders whenever possible to illustrate key concepts. The athletes quoted either currently train at Gold's Gym or have been headquartered at Gold's in the past.

You'll probably need to read this chapter two or three times before you feel confident that you have completely mastered all of the basic information we give you. And don't be surprised if some of the subjects discussed seem unclear to you until you've actually put them to practical use in a gym. Most novice bodybuilders find it difficult to master theoretical and practical information presented outside an actual gymnasium atmosphere.

If you find any of the topics discussed in this chapter to still be hazy after you've tried them out in the gym, you will find amplifying discussions of most topics in the two books previously published in this series, *The Gold's Gym Book of Bodybuilding* and *The Gold's Gym Training Encyclopedia*. Or if you have access to one, you can ask an experienced male or female bodybuilder for an in-person explanation of the subject.

There are limitations to discussing some of the finer points of bodybuilding in a book, so there are great advantages to having access to experienced bodybuilders. If nothing else, we may fail to anticipate and answer questions you might ask. And when this happens, we won't be there like an actual bodybuilder to answer your questions.

Whether you learn the basics of safe and productive bodybuilding training from this book or from some other source, you must understand each topic we discuss in this chapter before you begin serious training. If you fail to master all of these subjects early on, you increase the risk of incurring a disabling injury working out with weights.

TERMINOLOGY

An exhaustive glossary is included at the end of this book, and you should refer to it whenever you hear or read a term you don't understand. For now, however, we will define several of the most fundamental terms used in bodybuilding training.

The most basic unit of a bodybuilding workout is an *exercise*. An exercise is each individual bodybuilding movement performed, e.g., a Squat, Bench Press, Dumbbell Side Lateral, or Barbell Curl. It should come as no surprise to learn that an exercise is frequently called a *movement*.

As you perform an exercise, each full cycle of the movement—from the starting point through the full cycle of the exercise and back again to the starting point—is called a *repetition* or *rep*.

A collection of repetitions (usually 5–12) is called a *set*. Between sets a *rest interval* of 60–90 seconds is taken to allow fatigued muscles to partially recuperate before another set is initiated. You will normally do two or more sets of each bodybuilding exercise you perform.

When you are doing a set of an exercise, you will use a particular *weight* or *poundage* on the bar to place stress on the working muscles. And as your working muscles increase in hypertrophy you will be able to use progressively heavier poundages. A *limit* weight is the heaviest poundage you can move for one rep.

The complete list of exercises, sets, reps (and sometimes poundages) performed on one *training session* or *workout* is called a *routine*. A routine is sometimes called a *program* or *schedule*. Most frequently, a routine is presented in written form, as in a magazine article or training diary. And you can perform routines for your full body, or for individual muscle groups, in one workout.

When you physically perform a routine, you *train* or *work out*. And when you have completed the routine, you have finished a *workout* or *training session*.

While learning how to perform each exercise in chapters 3–6, it's essential that you understand which muscle(s) contract to move the weight. Otherwise, you wouldn't be able to mentally concentrate on the correct working muscle group as you perform a set of each exercise.

In Figure 2–1 on pages 12–13 you will find front, side, and back views of male and female bodybuilders with the names of each major muscle group identified. And in Figure 2–2 on pages 14–15, we present a chart of the function of each muscle group identified in Figure 2–1.

Scientifically speaking, the term for structure and location of muscle groups is *anatomy* and the term for function is *kinesiology*. You will most frequently hear experienced bodybuilders using these scientific terms rather than the more generic terms.

RESISTANCE PROGRESSION

In Chapter 1 we discussed how an overload placed on a muscle group induces hypertrophy. The secret to success in bodybuilding is to place a progressively greater overload on each skeletal muscle. And the best way to gradually increase the overload on a muscle is called resistance progression.

There are four commonly used methods of increasing the overload placed on a muscle group:

- Do a set number of repetitions, but use more weight than you handled the previous workout.
- Use the same weight as the previous workout, but do more repetitions.
- Maintain a consistent number of reps with a given weight, but increase the total number of sets performed for each exercise.
- Do the same number of sets and reps with the same weight as at a previous workout, but reduce the length of rest intervals between sets.

Advanced bodybuilders use all four of these methods of increasing the overload on a muscle group, but less experienced trainees use only the first two methods. As a novice in the sport, you will gradually increase the reps you do for a certain weight until you reach a predetermined level. Then you will add weight to the bar, decrease the number of repetitions you perform with the new weight, and begin to gradually work back up in reps.

If you look ahead to the training programs suggested at the end of the next chapter, you'll see a suggested repetition range for each exercise, e.g., 8–12. These are called *guide numbers*, with "8" being the *lower guide number* and "12" the *upper guide number*.

In a workout, you will begin an exercise with a certain weight for 8 reps, then add 1–2 repetitions to the movement each succeeding workout until you reach the upper guide number. Once you reach the upper guide number, add 5–20 pounds to the bar, drop back to the lower guide number for repetitions, and begin working up again in reps to the upper guide number.

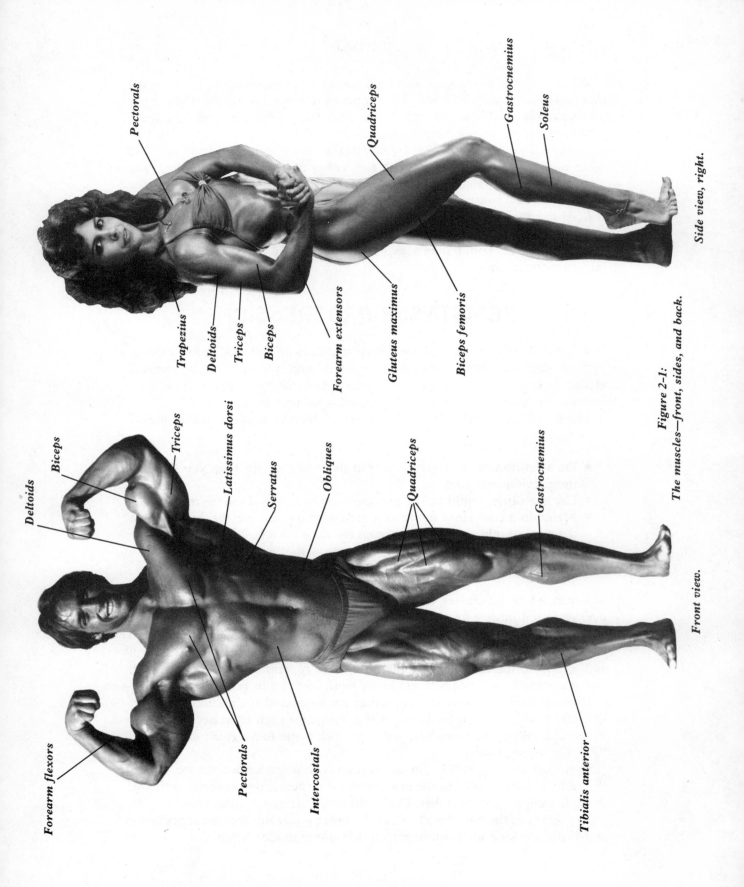

Pectorals

Trapezius

Deltoids

Triceps

Biceps

Forearm extensors

Quadriceps

Gluteus maximus

Biceps femoris

Gastrocnemius

Soleus

Side view, right.

Deltoids

Biceps

Triceps

Latissimus dorsi

Serratus

Obliques

Quadriceps

Gastrocnemius

Forearm flexors

Pectorals

Intercostals

Tibialis anterior

Front view.

*Figure 2-1:
The muscles—front, sides, and back.*

Deltoids

Triceps

Biceps

Serratus

Obliques

Gluteus maximus

Gastrocnemius

Tibialis anterior

Pectorals

Intercostals

Rectus Abdominis

Quadriceps

Soleus

Side view, left.

Forearm extensors

Trapezius

Erector Spinae

Gluteus Maximus

Deltoids

Brachialis

Latissimus Dorsi

Biceps femoris

Gastrocnemius

Back view.

Figure 2-2: Basic kinesiology for bodybuilders.

Muscle group	Popular Name	Location	Function	Typical exercises
Quadriceps	Quads	Front of thigh	Straightens leg from a fully bent position; helps to flex body at the waist.	Squats Leg Presses Leg Extensions
Biceps femoris	Hamstrings; thigh biceps	Back of thigh	Bends leg fully from a straightened position.	Stiff-Legged Deadlifts Leg Curls
Leg adductors		Inner thigh	Moves thighs inward toward each other.	Cable/Machine Adductions
Leg abductors		Outer thigh	Moves thighs away from each other.	Cable/Machine Abductions
Gluteus maximus	Glutes	Round part of tush	Help to straighten body from a position flexed at the waist	Squats Stiff-Legged Deadlifts
Gastrocnemius	Gastrocs; calves	Back of lower leg	Extends toes and foot when legs are straight or partially bent.	Standing Calf Raises
Soleus		Beneath the gastrocnemius	Extend toes and foot when leg is bent at a 90-degree angle.	Seated Calf Raises
Tibialis anterior		Front of lower leg	Flexes toes and foot.	Toe Raises
Erector spinae	Erectors; lumbars	Each side of spine from pelvis up to thorax	Helps to straighten body from a position fully flexed at waist; helps to arch back.	Deadlifts Hyperextensions Good Mornings
Latissimus dorsi	Lats	Outer parts of upper back	Pulls upper arm bones downward and to the rear; helps to arch back.	Chins Pulldowns Rows

Figure 2-3: *Example of simple progression.*

	Monday	Wednesday	Friday
Week 1	60 × 8	60 × 9	60 × 10
Week 2	60 × 11	60 × 12	65 × 8
Week 3	65 × 9	65 × 9	65 × 11
Week 4	65 × 12	70 × 8	70 × 9

Figure 2-4: *Example of complex progression.*

	Monday	Wednesday	Friday
Week 1	70 × 8	70 × 10	70 × 11
	70 × 8	70 × 9	70 × 9
	70 × 8	70 × 8	70 × 9
Week 2	70 × 12	70 × 12	70 × 12
	70 × 11	70 × 11	70 × 12
	70 × 9	70 × 10	70 × 11
Week 3	70 × 12	75 × 9	75 × 9
	70 × 12	75 × 8	75 × 8
	70 × 12	75 × 7	75 × 8
Week 4	75 × 10	75 × 11	75 × 11
	75 × 9	75 × 10	75 × 10
	75 × 8	75 × 8	75 × 10

4–6 months of steady training behind you. Only then will you be sufficiently experienced to profitably use cheating in your workouts."

Chris Glass (Los Angeles and California Women's Champion) elaborates, "Strict exercise form mandates moving only those parts of your body specified in an exercise performance description, plus being sure to move the weight over a complete range of motion. Cheating involves kicking with your legs, bending your torso backward, or otherwise imparting momentum to the weight. And short-range reps only rob your muscles of much of the developmental value of an exercise."

Charles Glass (National and World Middleweight Champion) concludes, "It takes strong mental concentration in order to maintain proper biomechanics in an exercise. You'll be more likely to cheat in a set when you allow your mind to wander. Poor concentration nearly always results in a less than optimum workout and a poor adaptive response by your skeletal muscles."

REST INTERVALS

The length of rest intervals taken between sets should be maintained at 60–90 seconds for beginning and intermediate bodybuilders. Training with longer pauses between sets can allow your body to cool down in mid-workout, increasing the risk of training injuries. And resting less than 60 seconds between sets won't allow sufficient recuperation time to permit a subsequent high-intensity set.

"The length of rest intervals between sets depends to a degree on which muscle group or groups you are training," asserts **Clare Furr**. "Exercises for large muscle groups like thighs, back, and chest or for more than one body part like Barbell Bent Rows for the lats, rear delts, and biceps burn up more oxygen than movements for smaller individual muscle groups. Therefore, you will need a longer rest interval between sets of Squats for your thighs, lower back, and buttocks than between sets of Dumbbell Concentration Curls for your biceps."

As you gain knowledge of bodybuilding and read more advanced books and magazine articles on training for the sport, you will learn that there are times when you might wish to rest 3–5 minutes between sets and other occasions when as little as 20–30 seconds rest between sets is more appropriate. However, you'll make better muscle mass and strength gains with less risk of injury if you stick to rest intervals of 60–90 seconds between sets at the beginning and intermediate levels of bodybuilding training.

BREATHING PATTERNS

It's a lot more important than you might think to maintain correct breathing patterns during a bodybuilding exercise. Breathing incorrectly in certain movements can actually be dangerous, so dangerous that your life could be in jeopardy if you breathe incorrectly.

Exercise physiologists have identified a phenomenon called the *Valsalva Effect* or *Valsalva Maneuver*. This effect involves holding your breath while lifting a very heavy poundage. If you hold your breath while exerting, blood flow to and from your brain is impeded, which in turn can cause you to faint. And if you happen to pass out when doing a heavy set of Bench Presses—and you haven't taken the precaution of having a spotter standing at the head end of the bench—the barbell can crash down on your exposed face and/or neck, causing serious injury and possibly even killing you.

"Don't take too lightly the dangers of passing out when doing heavy Bench Presses without a spotter," warns **Jeff Everson** (American Mixed Pairs Champion with his wife Corinna). "There are several well-documented cases of deaths occuring under just these circumstances. But at the same time you shouldn't be afraid of doing Bench Presses when you are careful to use a spotter and expel your breath while exerting to push the barbell upward. With the right safety precautions, the Bench Press is a very safe and productive exercise.''

The best rule for breathing during a set of a bodybuilding movement is to exhale as you exert during an exercise and inhale as you return the bar to the starting position of the exercise. Monitor this breathing pattern for two or three weeks, and correct breathing will become second nature to the point where you probably won't need to worry about it in future workouts. And, for emphasis, *never* hold your breath as you exert yourself in any exercise in your workout.

WORKOUT FREQUENCY

According to massive **Matt Mendenhall** (twice a runnerup in the Nationals), "Scientists have determined that muscles don't increase in hypertrophy until they have had sufficient time to recuperate following a heavy weight workout. And it takes at least 48 hours for the recuperation-hypertrophy process to take place. Therefore, you must allow at least one full day of rest between bodybuilding workout days for each muscle group.''

"At the beginning level of bodybuilding," **Corinna Everson** (American Champion, Ms. Olympia) feels, "you should train three nonconsecutive days each week. In order to leave your weekends free for family and recreational activities, the most common workout days are Monday, Wednesday, and Friday.'' With this scheme, you will have one full day of rest between each of the three workout days and two full days between cycles of workouts each week. So, this system allows you to recuperate fully between training sessions and induces your muscles to increase in mass and strength at the fastest possible speed.

"After 3–4 months of steady training, you can adopt a split routine training philosophy in which you work out more than three days per week," notes **Lou Ferrigno**. "With this system, you will work half of your body on Mondays and Thursdays and the other half on Tuesdays and Fridays, thereby allowing each muscle group plenty of time to recuperate between periods during which you stress the body part intensely with weights.''

RECUPERATION

"Even if you allow a full day of rest between workout days for each body part," warns **Dawn Marie Gnaegi** (U.S. Champion), "you can fail to fully recover if you don't get sufficient sleep each night or if you allow yourself to worry too much about life's occasional downers. In other words, insufficient sleep and excessive nervous energy drains can retard the recuperation process and prevent optimum progress from your workouts.''

"The amount of sleep you might require each night is highly individual," observes **Dr. Franco Columbu** (twice Mr. Olympia). "I suggest that you start with eight hours per night and observe how you feel the next day. If you find it difficult to get to sleep the following night, you require less than eight hours of sleep. But if you feel fatigued and sleepy the next day, you should attempt to sleep a bit more than eight hours the next night."

Stress can be quite harmful to the bodybuilding process. Excessive levels of stress can often be dissipated in a hard weight workout, but if you allow stress to rule your life you will have difficulty in making decent gains from your workouts. If stress is holding you back, try to develop a plan to reduce the amount of stress in your life.

The two best stress reduction methods are taking up a hobby that relaxes you and avoiding stressful situations. Or, you can use the suggestions in any of the many books on stress control that can be found in book stores.

Tina Plakinger (Ms. America and a leading IFBB pro bodybuilder) says, "Consistently failing to allow your body sufficient recuperation time between workouts is just as deadly to your bodybuilding efforts as consistently overdrawing your checking account can be to your financial rating. If you drive your body consistently into an energy debt, you will eventually become overtrained and will fail to make gains from your workouts, regardless of how hard you exert yourself."

If you are overtrained, you will exhibit one or more of the following eight symptoms:

- Lack of enthusiasm for workouts.
- Lack of pep and energy.
- Persistently sore joints and/or muscles.
- Insomnia.
- Loss of appetite.
- Elevated morning pulse rate.
- Elevated morning blood pressure.
- Deteriorated motor control.

If you conclude that you are overtrained, you should remedy the condition by first taking a one- or two-week layoff from bodybuilding workouts. You can continue aerobic exercise and physically demanding recreational activities if you like, but stay completely away from the gym during a layoff.

Once you are back in the gym, switch to a shorter and more intense routine. Normally, you will become overtrained from excessively long workouts rather than from highly intense training sessions, so doing shorter and more intense workouts is one of the best ways to avoid overtraining.

STARTING POUNDAGES

Relative starting weights for each exercise included in the basic routines in chapters 3–6 have been determined according to sex. They are expressed as percentages of bodyweight (see the "% Men" and "% Women" columns of each program).

Recommended starting poundages are based on average strength levels for men and women. But experience has taught us that few aspiring bodybuilders are "average." So if you are naturally stronger than normal and/or are in superior physical condition, suggested starting weights could be too light. And if you are particularly out of shape, they may be too heavy.

A weight is too heavy if you either can't reach the lower guide number for reps using it, or you must struggle to reach that number. The weight is excessively light if you can easily perform more than the upper guide number for repetitions. So after just a single workout with the suggested poundages, you will be able to confidently adjust them upward or downward by 5–10 pounds.

When you work out correct starting weights using the body weight percentages, it's best to always round downward to the nearest multiple of five pounds. So if you are a woman weighing 120 pounds, you should use 45 pounds for an exercise in which the suggested starting weight is 40% of your body weight. (The math is $120 \times 0.40 = 48.0$, which is rounded downward to 45 pounds.) At the beginners' level of bodybuilding, it's always better to use a weight that is too light than one that is too heavy.

WHAT TO WEAR

In the gym fashions can be highly individual. You should always wear shoes, but from that starting point you should consider only climatic conditions and personal preference when choosing what to wear for each workout.

"Running shoes are ideal for use in a bodybuilding workout," writes **Robby Robinson** (winner of many IFBB pro titles). "These shoes have built-in arch supports that protect your feet from compression injuries that might occur if you trained bare-footed. And the tred on running shoes allows you to securely grip a calf block with your toes and the balls of your feet when you perform calf exercises in a workout."

Athletic supporters for men and bras for women are strictly optional equipment in bodybuilding circles. So are stockings, although more Gold's Gym members wear socks than go without them.

"In hot weather, shorts and a t-shirt or tank top are appropriate workout attire," we learn from **Larry Jackson** (Mr. California). "But as the temperature in a gym drops, you should add warm-up pants and tops to your basic wardrobe. Generally speaking, several thin layers of clothing are warmer than one or two thick layers when the gym is cold. And you can easily discard one or two of the thinner layers as you get fully warmed up during a hard training session."

If perspiration tends to get into your eyes, you can wear either a baseball cap or headband. Or, you can carry a dry hand towel around the gym with you to periodically wipe off your face.

"Leather workout gloves have become popular with most hard-training bodybuilders," **Laura Combes** (American Champion) teaches us. "Gloves will protect your hands and prevent the buildup of excessive calluses. Alternatively, you can protect the palms of your hands with 4 × 4-inch squares of thin skin diving wetsuit rubber."

WHERE TO WORK OUT

This is a Gold's Gym book, so it should come as no surprise that we prefer to work out at the original Gold's Gym in Venice, California, or in one of the more than 100 other Gold's Gyms worldwide. This is one reason why we have established a policy of accepting visits from men and women with membership cards at any of the Gold's Gyms. But we realize that many readers won't have access to a Gold's Gym, so we will give you a hierarchical rating of various types of gyms in which you might choose to pump iron.

Other than a Gold's Gym, the best place in which you might work out is a serious bodybuilding gym. You can find listings of these gyms and other health clubs in the Yellow Pages of your telephone directory. Bodybuilding gyms are usually well-equipped, and they offer the best atmosphere for serious, purposeful bodybuilding workouts. You will also have access to the best bodybuilders in your area in this type of gym, which is a boon in terms of checking out your workout form and learning advanced training techniques.

One step down from bodybuilding gyms are school and YMCA weight rooms. This class of training facility varies widely in equipment complement, and the best gyms are as good as a Gold's Gym. But the less well-equipped gyms offer little to a serious bodybuilder.

Generally speaking, commercial health clubs and spas are an inferior choice for serious bodybuilders. As you continue training, you must keep pushing to use heavier weights with each succeeding month. Health clubs and spas seldom have heavy enough equipment for serious bodybuilders.

If you fully equip a home gym, you can easily get great workouts in your basement or garage *if* you have a training partner to spot you. With gym memberships costing more than $200 every year, a one-time investment of $400–$500 to completely equip a home gym makes good economic sense if you intend to stick with bodybuilding over the long haul.

On the negative side of the coin, home gym workouts can become lonely and boring, and you are stuck trying to figure out the finer points of the bodybuilding process on your own. As a result, we have found that even men and women with extensively equipped home gyms prefer to take many of their workouts at Gold's. The camaraderie and equipment inventory offered by a hardcore bodybuilding gym make it the ideal choice of exercise facility for all serious bodybuilders.

WHEN TO TRAIN

It's best to work out at the same time each training day because this practice encourages workout regularity. But it matters little physiologically which hour of the day you choose to pump iron.

Gold's Gym/Venice is open 24 hours a day, and there are dedicated bodybuilders using the facility at all hours. The hours of heaviest usage are between 7 and 10 in the morning and between 4 and 7 in the afternoon and early evening. But you can find champion bodybuilders like **Casey Viator** (history's youngest Mr. America and the winner of several IFBB Pro Grand Prix Championships) training at Gold's even in the middle of the night.

There is a little evidence that a bodybuilder's body prepares itself for an all-out energy expenditure at any time of the day when it is consistently stressed. If this theory eventually proves to be correct, it will be one more reason why you should train at the same time each workout day.

TRAINING PARTNERS

Some bodybuilders prefer to work out with a training partner, while others prefer pumping iron alone. **Lou Ferrigno** is typical of bodybuilders who like to use a partner: "I do a lot of forced reps in my workouts, which requires a training partner being there at all times. Close to a competition or important posing exhibition, a partner can help you to maintain the speedy workout pace that etches deep striations across each muscle group. And it's always easier to get an extra rep or two on my own at the end of a set when my partner is there to encourage me.

"The hard part about using a training partner is finding one who is motivated to train as hard and consistently as I do. Often a guy might think he will be able to keep up with me, but after two or three weeks he begs off with an injury or some other excuse. But once you find one, a good training partner is worth his or her weight in amino acid capsules!"

Tom Platz (Mr. Universe and a 3rd-place finisher in the Mr. Olympia competition) prefers a more solitary approach to his workouts: "When I have a training partner, I always seem to lose something from my own workouts, so I prefer to train alone. But I always need spotters for safety and to hand me heavy dumbbells weighing up to 180 pounds each, so I work out with other people around me in the gym."

You should always have a spotter standing by when you perform heavy Bench Presses and Squats, or at any time when you might decide to do forced reps. So even if you prefer to train alone, follow Tom Platz's advice and work out when there are other bodybuilders in the gym who will spare a moment of their time to spot you when you need it.

Chris Lund

Tom Platz.

RECORD KEEPING

"There are literally hundreds of different training and dietary variables that you can use in your personal bodybuilding philosophy," explains **Samir Bannout** (Mr. Olympia), "and each one will cause your unique body to react differently than anyone else's. Due to this individuality of reacting to external stimuli, you must experiment with as many of these variables as possible, in order to discover how best to train and feed your body to bring about the quickest results."

The easiest way to make order out of chaos in bodybuilding is to maintain a detailed training and dietary log book. You can keep these records in either commercially prepared diaries like *Joe Weider's* Muscle & Fitness *Training Diary* (Contemporary, 1982), or in any notebook or bound book with blank pages and a minimum degree of durability.

At the bottom end of the scale, you should at least record the date and time of each workout, along with the exercises you did, the weights you used, and the reps performed for each set. For this purpose you can use a form of bodybuilding shorthand that looks like this:

1) Bench Press: 135×10; 165×8; 185×6
2) Incline Dumbbell Press: $50 \times 8 \times 8 \times 7$

In the foregoing example, Bench Presses were performed for one set of 10 reps with 135 pounds, one set of eight with 165, and one set of six with 185. And Incline Dumbbell Presses were done with a pair of 50-pound dumbbells for three sets of eight, eight and seven reps.

In terms of diet, you should record the time of each meal, as well as the exact quantities of each food consumed. And you should always individually list every food supplement you take.

Other data that can find their way into your training diary include relative energy reserves, enthusiasm levels, amount of sleep you had the previous night, what inspired you for a workout, which factors in your life are causing stress, and any other factors that might have had an effect on the value of your workout.

SAFETY FACTORS

As mentioned earlier, bodybuilding training can be dangerous if certain safety rules are not followed. But if you follow the safety rules presented in this section, you never need fear your workouts. They'll be safe.

The best set of safety rules we have seen was outlined by **Lou Ferrigno**. Here are Louie's 12 safety suggestions:

1. *Use spotters.* This rule is particularly important when you are doing Bench Presses and Squats with very heavy poundages.

2. *Never train alone.* Even if you don't have a steady spotter, you can have a friend or family member stand in with you. Training alone can be dangerous.

Lou Ferrigno.

3. *Use catch racks.* If you can't round up a spotter, be sure to do heavy Benches and Squats with catch racks on which you can rest the bar if you don't have enough strength to move it up from the bottom position of the exercise.

4. *Use collars on the bar.* Should you fail to use collars on a barbell, one end might dip a little during the exercise, dumping the plates off that end. When this happens, the suddenly heavier opposite end will whip downward, which in turn can wrench your lower back, an ankle, a knee, or some other vulnerable joint.

5. *Never hold your breath.* This rule was discussed earlier. Holding your breath can make you pass out, leaving you open to serious injury when you fall or a bar crashes down on your body.

6. *Maintain good gym housekeeping.* Always pick up barbells and dumbbells lying on the floor and return them to appropriate racks. And keep loose plates and other equipment off the floor. It's easy to trip over weights lying on the floor, and you can fall against a piece of equipment and seriously injure yourself.

7. *Train under competent supervision.* Most gyms have instructors and/or a manager who can monitor your exercise form and spot potential danger points in your routine. If you fail to correct training errors early in your bodybuilding experience, they will become bad habits that will be almost impossible to change.

8. *Don't work out in an overcrowded gym.* If you train in a gym that is so crowded that you must wait for a piece of equipment, your body can cool off and leave you open to injury. It would be much better for you to choose another time of the day to train when the gym is less crowded.

9. *Always warm up thoroughly.* We talk about the importance of warming up to prevent training injuries later in this chapter. And once you are warmed up, you must keep warm by training at a fairly quick pace.

10. *Use proper biomechanics.* Safe and correct exercise form is explained in the exercise performance descriptions in chapters 3–6. As long as you follow the instructions to the letter, you won't expose your body to unwarranted stresses that might cause an injury.

11. *Use a weightlifting belt.* This broad leather belt protects your lower back and abdomen from injuries when you do limit sets of Squats, overhead lifts, and heavy back exercises. Cinched tightly around your waist, a weightlifting belt protects your unstable midsection by bracing it firmly.

12. *Acquire as much knowledge as possible about bodybuilding training.* When you know everything possible about bodybuilding, you are able to avoid potentially injurious situations, so you should constantly read all of the bodybuilding magazines and books you can find to improve and update your knowledge of the bodybuilding process.

SELF-EVALUATION

Whether you wish one day to compete as a bodybuilder, or merely wish to have a nice body, it's essential that you periodically evaluate your progress in the sport. You should particularly try to identify muscle groups that are lagging behind the remainder of your body so you can apply greater training intensity to the weak points and bring them back into line with the rest of your physique.

If you're shooting for a well-toned physique without the extreme muscle mass of a competitive bodybuilder, you should still try to avoid noticeably under- or overdeveloped muscle groups. You'll look ridiculous, for example, if you allow your upper body to become so massive in comparison to your spindly legs that you end up reminding people of a seagull at the beach!

It's even more important to maintain harmonious body proportions from the first weeks of your bodybuilding involvement if you intend eventually to compete. One of the first qualities judges look for in a competition is proportional balance. And the longer you fail to work on a weak point, the more likely it becomes that you'll *never* get that lagging body part up to the level of the rest of your physique.

Tim Belknap tells you how to determine if you have balanced physical proportions: "All bodybuilders—male and female alike—quickly develop a good sense of proportional balance by viewing the photos of top bodybuilders publicized each month in *Muscle & Fitness, Flex, MuscleMag International, Iron Man,* and all the other bodybuilding magazines available on newsstands.

"For many bodybuilders it's difficult to evaluate one's own physique, particularly if a mirror is used as the only guide. If you tend to magnify your strong points and ignore your weaknesses in front of a mirror, you should have photos taken of yourself in a variety of poses each 6–8 weeks. It's much easier to objectively evaluate your physique in photos than it is in front of a mirror with a friendly overhead light.

"If you still have difficulty detecting weak points that demand special attention, you should seek the critical advice of a competition judge, an experienced competitor, or a wise gym owner. But be sure to approach any of these people—especially a judge—with an obvious willingness to accept an outside opinion. Nothing will eliminate a valuable critic faster than you exploding, 'What do you mean bad calves?!! My calves are great. Just look at them!'

"You should take evaluations from your friends with a grain of salt, because it's usually impossible for friends and family to analyze your physique objectively. You could look like you've been eating glazed doughnuts three meals a day for a year, and a friend or family member will still think you're ripped to shreds. You don't need this kind of advice; it's far better to receive harsh criticism."

PROGRAM BREAK-IN

You should break slowly and gradually into a full bodybuilding routine. If you jump into a full program, your muscles will be so sore a day after your first workout that you may wish you were dead. And the less physically active you've been prior to initiating a bodybuilding program, the more slowly you should break yourself in, because weight training is a far more intense form of exercise than anything you've done previously.

For your initial workout, you should first warm up, then perform only one set of each exercise listed in Level One programs in chapters 3–6. Multiple sets will be listed for most exercises in these routines, but you should still perform only one set per movement for your first two workouts.

When you do your third and fourth workouts, you can move up to two sets of each exercise for which two or more sets are recommended. And from your fifth workout, you can safely and confidently perform the full routine.

Unless a weight feels ludicrously light to you the first few workouts, you should avoid deliberately increasing workout poundages prior to the beginning of your third week of training. You will experience muscle soreness from initiating training too heavily just as easily as you can become sore from too lengthy a training session.

Even if you religiously follow the forgoing break-in program, you might experience mild to moderate muscle soreness. We have heard of many remedies to muscle soreness, but the only effective method in our experience is a long, hot bath repeated 2–3 times a day if pain persists.

WARMING UP

It's absolutely essential that you warm up thoroughly without weights before tackling heavy iron in your workouts. A good warm-up can help prevent training injuries, allow you to handle heavier workout weights, and fine tune motor coordination prior to a hard training session. These functions of a preworkout warm-up have been verified by both American and Soviet scientists and empirically proven by thousands of bodybuilders worldwide.

A good warm-up should consist of light aerobic activity, calisthenics, and stretching for 10–15 minutes before a weight workout. Your warm-up should be continued until you break a sweat, so it stands to reason that you won't need as long a workout in the summer as your body requires when the weather is colder.

The warm-up that we recommend consists of the following activities done in the order presented:

Running in Place. Begin with a slow cadence, barely lifting your feet from the floor and slowly increase the cadence, lifting your knees higher and higher. Take 3–5 minutes to build up to a fast pace and an exaggerated leg movement.

Back and Hamstrings Stretch. Position your feet a little wider than your shoulders and hold your legs straight throughout the exercise. Bend forward and grasp your right ankle, pulling your torso downward until you feel a stretching sensation in your hamstrings. Hold this position for about 30 seconds. Repeat the stretch to the opposite ankle.

Freehand Squats. Place your feet about shoulder-width apart and extend your arms straight forward from your shoulders throughout the movement. Keeping your torso upright, slowly bend your knees and sink into a full squatting position. Return to the starting point and repeat the movement for 15–20 repetitions with a slow cadence.

Shoulder Stretch. Grasp the ends of a towel in your hands and extend your arms directly upward in a "V" from your shoulders. Keep tension on the towel and keep your arms straight while you move your hands backward and downward in semicircular arcs until your shoulders "dislocate" and the towel comes to rest against the back of your thighs. Return to the starting position and repeat the movement for 3–5 repetitions.

Running in place.

Back and Hamstring Stretch.

Freehand Squat.

All warm-up photos by Bill Reynolds

Shoulder Stretch (or Shoulder Dislocate)—start, left; finish, below.

Jumping Jacks, start/finish.

Jumping Jacks, midpoint.

Push-Ups, finish.

Jumping Jacks. This rhythmic movement begins with your feet together and arms down at your sides while standing erect. Bend your knees slightly and forcefully straighten them to spring into the air. Simultaneously raise your arms directly out to the sides and upward until they touch and spread your legs apart so you land with your feet placed a bit wider than your shoulders. Bend your knees to absorb the shock of landing, then immediately spring back into the air and return to the starting position. Repeat the movement rhythmically for 20–30 repetitions.

Push-Ups. Everyone has done Push-Ups at one time or another. Do 10–20 repetitions as part of your warm-up. Weaker individuals can do the movement resting on their knees rather than their toes.

Calf Stretches. Stand facing a wall with your toes 2½–3 feet from the wall. Lean forward and place your hands about shoulder-width apart on the wall just below shoulder level. Straighten your arms and body, then force your heels toward the floor to stretch your calves. You can also do this stretch with one leg at a time. If you can place your heels flat on the floor without fully stretching your calves, you should step backward 6–8 more inches to place yourself in a better position to stretch the muscle group.

Calf Stretch.

Torso Stretch, start.

Torso Stretch, finish.

Torso Stretch. Assume the same starting position as for Push-Ups. Keeping your arms straight throughout the exercise, first raise your hips as far from the floor as possible. Then lower them as close to the floor as you can or even rest them on the floor. Throw your head back in this position. Move back to the position with your hips high and repeat the movement.

IN THE GYM

Before we send you into the gym to actually work out, we wish to emphasize the vital importance of not missing scheduled workouts. One of the most common reasons for slow progress in bodybuilding is inconsistent training, so you *must* train with clockwork regularity if you truly wish to make good progress as a bodybuilder.

Lou Ferrigno.

3
TRAINING WITH FREE WEIGHTS

The definition of free weights includes barbells, dumbbells, and related resistance equipment used to increase strength and improve muscular development. Free weights have been in relatively common use for more than a century longer than Universal, Nautilus, or any of the many brands of exercise machines found in well-equipped gyms. And free weights are in far more common use than any brand of resistance exercise machine.

During the middle of the 19th century, barbells consisted of solid globes attached to the ends of an iron bar. The first dumbbells were of similar construction, but they were so ponderous that most strength athletes did very little work with them.

Early barbells weren't adjustable in weight, so a bodybuilder or weightlifter needed a set of 10–15 barbells of different poundages to permit a proper workout. Then during the late 1800s, a barbell with hollow globes evolved, permitting a time-consuming weight adjustment by inserting or removing varying quantities of lead shot.

The fertile mind of Allan Calvert created the first adjustable barbell/dumbbell set early in the 20th century. This plate-loading apparatus has been periodically updated over the years, but Calvert's basic design has remained in use for three-quarters of a century. In fact, you will use Calvert's barbells and dumbbells in all of the free-weight workouts presented in this chapter.

ADVANTAGES AND DISADVANTAGES

Compared to exercise machines, free weights are very inexpensive. A Universal machine costs several times the $500 or so required to set up a complete free-weight home gym, while a Nautilus layout sufficient to work each muscle group costs many times as much as a Universal machine.

It's often boring to train on machines because they limit you to only 3–4 exercises per muscle group. In contrast, we could give you a minimum of 10–15 movements for each body part using free weights and related equipment. We present only a few of these exercises in this chapter, so you should consult our previous book, *The Gold's Gym Encyclopedia of Training,* for a more complete list of free-weight movements for each muscle group.

The main disadvantage of training with free weights is that they have more potential for injury than exercise machines. But if you follow the safety rules presented in Chapter 2, you can make free-weight workouts equally as safe as training sessions on various machines.

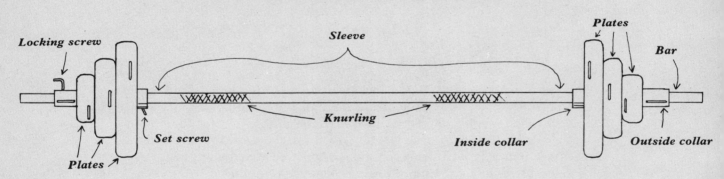

Figure 3–1: Illustrated terminology of a barbell.

EQUIPMENT ORIENTATION

In Figure 3–1 above, you will find a drawing of a barbell with each of its parts identified. Dumbbells differ from barbells only in terms of length, being 10–14 inches long compared to the 4- to 6-foot length of most barbells. The terminology of a dumbbell is identical to the terminology of a barbell.

Plates can be made from either metal or vinyl-covered concrete. Metal plates are more durable and you can load a bar with a much greater poundage using the thinner cast iron plates. On the other hand, vinyl-covered plates are less harmful to wooden or linoleum floors.

Barbells and dumbbells can come with or without a hollow metal sleeve, which allows the bar to rotate more freely in your hands. Either the sleeve or the bar handle is scored with crosshatched grooves called *knurlings,* which give you a more secure grip on the bar when your hands are sweaty.

Barbells and dumbbells can be either fixed (as found in most commercial gyms) or adjustable (as in most sets used at home). Adjustable barbells and dumbbells have removable collars which allow you to add or subtract plates to arrive at the desired poundage for an exercise. Fixed weights have the collars bolted or welded permanently in place to fix the bar at a certain poundage. Commercial gyms have racks and racks of fixed barbells and dumbbells in 5- to 10-pound increments from light to heavy poundages.

There is a specialized form of barbell called an Olympic barbell, which is used in weightlifting and powerlifting competitions, as well as for heavy movements in bodybuilding workouts. This barbell has a standard internationally accepted design, so there is little variation between Olympic barbells in Los Angeles and Olympic barbells in Moscow. An unloaded Olympic bar weighs 45 pounds or 20 kilograms (44½ lbs.). Collars weigh 5 pounds or 2½ kilos (5½ lbs.). The weights of these parts of the bar must be taken into consideration when adjusting the bar to the correct poundage for an exercise.

Generally speaking, barbells are used for heavy basic exercises stressing all parts of the body. Dumbbells are used for lighter isolation work on all parts of the body. Barbells primarily build mass and power, while dumbbells add shape and detail to your physique.

There is a wide variety of benches, leg machines, pulleys, chinning bars, dipping bars, and other apparati used in conjuction with free weights in a bodybuilding workout. Each of these pieces of supplementary equipment has a unique function, which will become clear to you as you read the exercise descriptions in this chapter, plus those in the two previous books in this series.

SUGGESTED FREE-WEIGHT EXERCISES

Twenty-seven key free-weight movements are fully described and illustrated in this section. To correctly learn each new movement, you should first read the exercise description while looking at the photos illustrating the movement. Mentally track the exercise, then try it with a light weight, and finally do the movement with a heavy poundage.

ABDOMINAL EXERCISES

SIT-UPS

Stress points: Front abdominals, particularly the upper half of the rectus abdominis muscle wall.

1. Lie down on an abdominal board with your feet toward the upper end.
2. Hook your toes and insteps beneath the roller pads or strap at the top end of the board.
3. Bend your legs at 45-degree angles and keep them bent throughout the exercise.

Sit-Ups, start.

4. Place your hands behind your head and neck.
5. Use only abdominal strength to curl your torso off the board, raising first your head, then shoulders followed by upper back, mid-back, and lower back, until your torso is perpendicular to the surface of the board.
6. Reverse the procedure and slowly lower your torso back to the starting point.
7. Repeat the movement for the required number of repetitions.

Sit-Ups, finish.

BENCH LEG RAISES

Stress points: Front abdominals, particularly the lower half of the rectus abdominis muscle wall.

1. Lie back on a flat exercise bench with your hips at one end of the bench.
2. Reach behind your head and grasp the edges of the bench to steady your body in position throughout your set.
3. Either press your legs together or cross your ankles throughout the set.
4. Bend your legs slightly and keep them bent throughout your set.
5. Raise your heels about two inches from the floor.
6. Slowly raise your feet in a semicircular arc from the starting point up to a position directly above your hips.
7. Slowly lower your feet back to the starting point.
8. Repeat the movement for the suggested number of reps.

Bench Leg Raises, start.

Bench Leg Raises, finish. Note different grips used to steady lift.

SEATED TWISTING

Stress points: External oblique muscles on the sides of your waist.
1. Sit in the middle of a flat exercise bench with your legs straddling the bench.
2. Brace your ankles and lower legs against the upright legs of the bench to prevent your hips and legs from moving.
3. Rest a broomstick or unloaded barbell bar across your shoulders, wrapping your arms around the bar or stick.
4. Twist your torso as far to the right as possible.
5. Immediately twist as far to the left as possible.
6. Continue the movement rhythmically from one side to the other until you have done the assigned number of reps to each side.

Seated Twisting.

Seated Twisting.

HIP AND THIGH EXERCISES

SQUATS

Stress points: Quadriceps, buttocks, lower back, hamstrings, and abdominals; squatting also improves your BMR (basal metabolic rate).

1. Place a loaded barbell on a squat rack.
2. Step under the bar and position it across your shoulders, balancing it in position by holding the bar out near the plates.
3. Straighten your legs to remove the bar from the rack and step back one pace.
4. Place your feet about shoulder-width apart, your toes angled slightly outward.
5. Stiffen your back and tense your abdominal muscles to keep your torso upright during the movement.
6. Bending only your knees, slowly lower your body down into a full squatting position.
7. Without bouncing in the bottom position, slowly straighten your legs and return to the starting point of the movement.
8. Repeat the movement for an appropriate number of repetitions.

Squats—start, opposite page; finish, right.

LEG PRESSES

Stress points: Quadriceps, buttocks, hamstrings.
1. Sit down in an angled leg press machine with your butt and back against the angled back rest and your tush resting on the padded seat.
2. Place your feet about shoulder-width on the sliding platform of the machine and straighten your legs.
3. Rotate the stop bars at the sides of your hips to release the sliding platform for the movement.
4. Slowly bend your legs as completely as possible.
5. Slowly straighten your legs.
6. Repeat the movement for the desired number of reps.
7. Rotate the stop bars back into the locked position at the end of your set and bring the platform gently down to rest against the stops.

Leg Presses (Angled), start.

Leg Presses, finish.

LEG EXTENSIONS

Stress points: Quadriceps.

1. Sit in a leg extension machine with the backs of your knees against the edge of the padded surface toward the lever arm of the apparatus.
2. Hook your toes and insteps under the lower set of roller pads (if there are two sets).
3. Grasp the handles provided at the sides near your hips or the edge of the padded surface of the machine to steady your upper body during your set.

Leg Extensions, start.

4. Moving only your knees, slowly straighten your legs under the resistance provided by the machine.
5. Hold the top position of the movement (legs straight) for a slow count of two.
6. Slowly lower your feet back to the starting point.
7. Repeat the movement for the required number of reps.

Leg Extensions, finish.

LEG CURLS

Stress points: Hamstrings.

1. Lie facedown on the flat surface of a leg curl machine, your knees placed on the edge of the pad toward the lever arm of the apparatus.
2. Hook your heels under the upper set of roller pads (if there are two sets).
3. Grasp the handles provided at the sides of the pad, or the padded edges of the machine to steady your torso in position during your set.
4. Press your hips against the pad and keep them in this position throughout the set.
5. Moving only your knees, slowly bend your legs as fully as possible under the resistance provided by the machine.
6. Hold the top position of the movement (legs fully bent) for a slow count of two.
7. Slowly lower your feet back to the starting point.
8. Repeat the movement for the suggested number of repetitions.

Leg Curls, start.

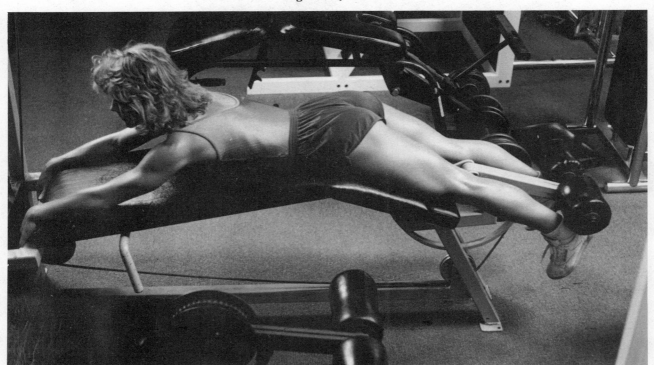

Leg Curls, finish.

BACK EXERCISES

DEADLIFTS

Stress points: Erector spinae, quadriceps, hamstrings, buttocks, forearm flexors, trapezius, latissimus dorsi muscles.

1. Load a barbell lying on the floor with a heavy weight.
2. Step up to the bar with your feet about shoulder-width apart and your shins touching the bar.
3. Bend over and take a shoulder-width overgrip on the bar (palms toward your legs).

Deadlifts, start.

4. Bend your legs, flatten your back, lower your hips, and straighten your arms to assume the starting position illustrated.
5. Lift the weight off the floor by first straightening your legs and then straightening your back until you are standing erect and the bar is resting across your upper thighs.
6. Lower the barbell slowly back to the floor by reversing the procedure used to raise it.
7. Repeat the movement for an appropriate number of reps.

Deadlifts, finish.

BARBELL BENT ROWS

Stress points: Latissimus dorsi, trapezius, spinal erectors, rear deltoids, biceps, brachialis, forearm flexors.

1. Load a moderately heavy poundage on a barbell lying on the floor.
2. Set your feet about shoulder-width apart approximately one foot back from the barbell.
3. Take a shoulder-width overgrip on the barbell.
4. Bend your legs slightly and keep them bent throughout the set.

Barbell Bent Rows, start.

5. Straighten your arms and flatten your back, raising your back to a position parallel to the floor. (The barbell should be free of the floor in this position.)
6. Moving only your arms, bend your arms and pull the barbell directly upward to touch your lower ribcage or upper abdomen.
7. Hold this top position of the movement momentarily.
8. Slowly lower the weight back to the starting point.
9. Repeat the exercise for the stated number of reps.

Barbell Bent Rows, finish.

SEATED PULLEY ROWS

Stress points: Latissimus dorsi, trapezius, spinal erectors, rear deltoids, biceps, brachialis, forearm flexors.

1. Attach a handle to the end of a cable running through the low pulley apparatus that gives you a narrow, parallel-hands grip.
2. Grasp the pulley with your palms facing each other, place your feet against the stop bar at the front of the apparatus, and sit down on the bench.
3. Bend your legs slightly and keep them bent throughout your set.

Seated Pulley Rows, start.

4. Straighten your arms and lean forward at the waist to fully stretch your upper back muscles.
5. Keeping your upper arms in at your sides, simultaneously sit erect and pull the handle toward your torso to touch lightly against your upper abdomen.
6. Arch your back in the finish position of the movement and hold this position for a moment.
7. Reverse the procedure and return to the starting point of the exercise.
8. Repeat the movement for the required number of reps.

Seated Pulley Rows, finish.

LAT MACHINE PULLDOWNS

Stress points: Latissimus dorsi, rear deltoids, biceps, brachialis, forearm flexors.

1. Take an overgrip on a lat machine handle with your hands set about 3–4 inches wider than your shoulders on each side.
2. Straighten your arms and sit down on the seat beneath the lat pulley, wedging your knees under the restraint bar to keep your body in position during the movement.
3. Arch your spine throughout the set, particularly at the finish position of the movement.
4. Keeping your elbows back, bend your arms and pull the lat bar down to a position touching your trapezius muscles behind your neck. (Alternatively, you can pull the bar down to touch your upper chest in front of your neck, or pull reps alternately to the front and back of your neck.)
5. Hold this finish position of the exercise for a moment.
6. Straighten your arms to return to the starting position.
7. Repeat the movement for the suggested number of repetitions.

Lat Machine Pulldowns, start.

Lat Machine Pulldowns,
finish (behind neck).

Lat Machine Pulldowns,
finish (before neck).

BARBELL SHRUGS

Stress points: Trapezius, deltoids, forearm flexors.
1. Load a barbell lying on the floor with a moderately heavy weight, then deadlift it up to your waist.
2. Keeping your arms straight throughout the movement, sag your shoulders forward and downward as fully as you can.
3. Shrug your shoulders upward and to the rear as far as possible.
4. Hold the top point of the movement for a moment.
5. Lower slowly back to the starting point with the bar across your upper thighs and your shoulders moved forward and downward.
6. Repeat the movement for the desired number of reps.

Barbell Shrugs—start, right; finish, opposite page.

SHOULDER EXERCISES

STANDING PRESSES

Stress points: Anterior-medial deltoids, triceps, upper pectorals, trapezius, and those upper back muscles that impart rotational force to the scapulae.

1. Load a barbell lying on the floor with a moderate weight.
2. Set your feet about shoulder-width apart and bend over to take a shoulder-width grip on the barbell.
3. Dip your hips, flatten your back, and clean the weight to your shoulders.
4. Rotate your elbows to a position beneath the bar.
5. Keeping your torso upright, slowly push the weight directly upward until it reaches straight arm's length directly above your head.
6. Slowly lower the barbell back to your shoulders.
7. Repeat the movement for the correct number of reps.

Standing Press, start.

Standing Press, finish.

DUMBBELL SIDE LATERALS

Stress points: Medial-anterior deltoids, trapezius, and those upper back muscles that impart rotational force to the scapulae.

1. Grasp two light dumbbells and stand erect with your arms down at your sides.
2. Bend your arms slightly and keep them bent throughout your set.
3. Rotate your hands so your palms face each other and press the dumbbells together about four inches in front of your hips.

Dumbbell Side Laterals, start.

Dumbbell Side Laterals, finish.

4. Bend slightly forward at the waist and maintain this torso position.
5. Using only deltoid strength, raise the dumbbells in semicircular arcs out to the sides and slightly forward until they reach shoulder height. (Be sure to keep your palms toward the floor throughout the movement.)
6. Hold this top position for a moment.
7. Lower the dumbbells slowly back along the same arcs to the starting point.
8. Repeat the movement for the required number of reps.

DUMBBELL BENT LATERALS

Stress points: Posterior deltoids, trapezius.
1. Grasp two light dumbbells and set your feet about shoulder-width apart.
2. Bend over so your torso is parallel with the floor throughout the set.
3. Bend your arms slightly and keep them bent.
4. Rotate your hands so your palms face each other and press the dumbbells together directly beneath your chest.

Dumbbell Bent Laterals, start.

5. Keeping your palms toward the floor, raise the weights in semicircular arcs directly out to the sides until they are at shoulder level.
6. Hold this top position of the movement for a moment.
7. Lower the dumbbells slowly back to the starting point.
8. Repeat the movement for an appropriate number of reps.

Dumbbell Bent Laterals, finish.

UPRIGHT ROWS

Stress points: Medial–posterior deltoids, trapezius, biceps, brachialis, forearm flexors.

1. Take a narrow overgrip in the middle of a barbell handle, your index fingers set about six inches apart.
2. Place your feet about shoulder-width apart, your arms running straight down from your shoulders and the bar resting in your hands across your upper thighs.

Upright Rows, start.

3. Bend your arms and pull the barbell directly upward close to your body, until your hands touch your chin. (Be sure to keep your elbows above the level of your hands throughout the set.)
4. Hold this top position of the movement for a moment.
5. Lower the weight slowly back to the starting point.
6. Repeat the movement for the listed number of reps.

Upright Rows, finish.

CHEST EXERCISES

BENCH PRESSES

Stress points: Pectorals, anterior–medial deltoids, triceps, latissimus dorsi, and those upper back muscles that impart rotational force to the scapulae.

1. Place a loaded barbell on the support rack of a pressing bench.
2. Lie back on the bench with your shoulders about six inches from the rack and your feet flat on the floor.
3. Take an overgrip on the barbell handle, your hands set 3–4 inches wider than your shoulders on each side.

Bench Press, start.

4. Straighten your arms to lift the weight from the rack to a supported position directly above your shoulders.
5. Being sure that your upper arms travel directly out to the sides, bend your arms, and slowly lower the barbell downward to lightly touch the middle of your chest.
6. Without bouncing the bar off your chest, straighten your arms to press the weight back to the starting point.
7. Repeat the movement for the desired number of repetitions.

Bench Press, finish.

INCLINE PRESSES/DECLINE PRESSES

Stress points: Inclines stress the upper pectorals, anterior-medial deltoids, and triceps; Declines stress the lower-outer pectorals, anterior-medial deltoids, and triceps.

1. Place a loaded barbell on the support rack of either bench.
2. Lie back on the incline or decline bench.
3. Take an overgrip on the barbell handle, your hands set 3–4 inches wider than your shoulders on each side.

Incline Press, finish.

Incline Press, start.

4. Straighten your arms to lift the weight from the rack to a supported position directly above your shoulders.
5. Being sure that your upper arms travel directly out to the sides, bend your arms to slowly lower the barbell downward to lightly touch your upper chest (Inclines) or lower chest (Declines).
6. Without bouncing the bar off your chest, straighten your arms to press the weight back to the starting point.
7. Repeat the movement for the suggested number of reps.

Decline Press, start.

Decline Press, finish.

DUMBBELL FLYES

Stress points: Incline Flyes stress the upper pectorals and anterior–medial deltoids; Flat-Bench Flyes stress the entire mass of the pectorals and the anterior–medial deltoids; Decline Flyes stress the lower-outer pectorals and the anterior–medial deltoids.

1. Grasp a moderately heavy pair of dumbbells and lie back on an incline, flat or decline bench.
2. Push the dumbbells upward to straight arms' length and rotate your wrists so your palms face each other.

Dumbbell Flyes, start.

Dumbbell Flyes, finish. Note that these are done on an incline bench.

3. Bend your arms slightly to remove potentially harmful stress from your elbows and keep them bent throughout your set.
4. Moving your arms directly out to the sides, slowly lower the dumbbells in semicircular arcs until they are below the level of your chest.
5. Use pectoral strength to raise the dumbbells back along the same arcs to the starting point.
6. Repeat the movement for the required number of reps.

Flat-Bench Dumbbell Flyes, finish.

Decline Dumbbell Flyes, finish.

ARM EXERCISES

STANDING BARBELL CURLS

Stress points: Biceps, forearm flexors.
1. Take an undergrip on a barbell handle, your hands set slightly wider than your shoulders.
2. Set your feet about shoulder-width apart and stand erect, your arms running straight down at your sides and the barbell resting across your upper thighs.

Standing Barbell Curl, start.

3. Press your upper arms against the sides of your chest and keep them in this position throughout the movement.
4. Fully straighten your arms.
5. Keeping your wrists straight or slightly flexed, use biceps strength to curl barbell from your thighs to a point directly beneath your chin.
6. Slowly lower the barbell back along the same arc to the starting point.
7. Repeat the movement for an appropriate number of repetitions.

Standing Barbell Curl, finish.

ALTERNATE DUMBBELL CURLS

Stress points: Biceps, forearm flexors.
1. Grasp two moderately weighted dumbbells.
2. Set your feet about shoulder-width apart and stand erect, your arms running down your sides and your palms toward your thighs.
3. Press your upper arms against the sides of your chest and keep them in this position throughout the movement.
4. Fully straighten your arms.
5. Keeping your wrists straight or slightly flexed, use biceps strength to curl the weight in your left hand upward along a semicircular arc to your shoulder.

Alternate Dumbbell Curl, start.

6. Be sure to rotate your wrist so your palms are facing upward during the second half of the movement.
7. Reverse the procedure to lower the wrist back to the starting point.
8. As you lower the weight in your left hand, begin to curl the weight in your right hand upward, using the same procedure as you used to curl the weight in your left hand.
9. Repeat the movement in seesaw fashion until you have completed the suggested number of repetitions with each arm.

Alternate Dumbbell Curl, finish.

PULLEY PUSHDOWNS

Stress points: Triceps, particularly the outer head of the muscle complex.
1. With your feet set about shoulder-width apart, stand facing an overhead pulley with a short bar handle attached to it.
2. Take an overgrip on the handle, your index fingers no more than 4–5 inches apart.

Pulley Pushdowns, start.

3. With your arms fully bent, press your upper arms against the sides of your ribcage and keep them in this position throughout the set.
4. Lean slightly forward at the waist.
5. Without moving your torso, slowly straighten your arms.
6. Slowly return the lat machine handle to the starting point.
7. Repeat the movement for an appropriate number of reps.

Pulley Pushdowns, finish.

LYING TRICEPS EXTENSIONS

Stress points: Triceps, particularly the inner head of the muscle group.
1. Take a narrow overgrip in the middle of a barbell handle, no more than 4–5 inches of space showing between your index fingers.
2. Lie back on a flat exercise bench with your feet set flat on the floor.
3. Extend your arms directly upward from your shoulders.

Lying Triceps Extension,
start.

4. Keep your upper arms motionless throughout your set.
5. Bend your arms and slowly lower the weight in a semicircular arc to the rear and downward until it lightly touches your forehead.
6. Use triceps strength to slowly push the barbell back up along the same arc to the starting point.
7. Repeat the movement for the desired number of reps.

Lying Triceps Extension,
finish.

BARBELL WRIST CURLS/BARBELL REVERSE WRIST CURLS

Stress points: Wrist Curls stress the forearm flexor muscles; Reverse Wrist Curls stress the forearm extensor muscles.

1. Take a shoulder-width undergrip (Wrist Curls) or overgrip (Reverse Wrist Curls) on a moderately weighted barbell.
2. Sit down at the end of a flat exercise bench with your feet set flat on the floor about shoulder-width apart.

Barbell Wrist Curl, start.

Barbell Wrist Curl, finish.

3. Run your forearms down your thighs with your wrists and hands off the edges of your knees as illustrated.
4. Sag your fists downward as far as possible.
5. Use forearm strength to raise the barbell in a small semicircular arc as high as possible.
6. Lower the weight slowly back to the starting point.
7. Repeat the movement for an appropriate number of repetitions.

Barbell Reverse Wrist Curl, start.

Barbell Reverse Wrist Curl, finish.

CALF EXERCISES

STANDING CALF RAISES

Stress points: Gastrocnemius muscles.
1. Stand facing a standing calf machine.
2. Place your toes and the balls of your feet on the toe block.
3. Bend your legs and position your shoulders under the yokes of the machine.

Standing Calf Raises, start.

4. Straighten your body to bear the weight of the machine.
5. Relax your calves to stretch your heels as far below the level of your toes as possible.
6. Rise up as high as you can on your toes.
7. Lower yourself slowly back to the starting point.
8. Repeat the movement for an appropriate number of repetitions.

Standing Calf Raises, finish.

SEATED CALF RAISES

Stress points: Soleus and gastrocnemius muscles.
1. Adjust the height of the knee pad assembly by removing the pin in it and replacing the pin.
2. Place your toes and the balls of your feet on the toe plate and slip the pads over your knees.
3. Push down with your toes and release the stop bar by pushing it forward.
4. Sag your heels as far below the level of your toes as possible.
5. Rise up on your toes as high as possible.
6. Return to the starting point.
7. Repeat the movement for the required number of reps.
8. Replace the stop bar at the end of your set.

Adjusting knee pad assembly for proper height.

Seated Calf Raises, start.

Seated Calf Raises, finish.

CALF PRESSES

Stress points: Gastrocnemius muscles.
1. Assume the starting position for Leg Presses.
2. Slide your heels off the platform until just your toes and the balls of your feet are in contact with it.
3. Allow your toes to move as close to your body as possible.
4. Push with your toes to extend your feet fully.
5. Return to the starting point.
6. Repeat the movement for the desired number of reps.

Calf Press (Angled), start.

Calf Press, finish.

SUGGESTED FREE-WEIGHT ROUTINES

The four training programs outlined on these pages can be used in the sequence presented, spending 4–6 weeks on each one. If you have never trained with weights before, be sure to use the gradual break-in procedure explained in Chapter 2 with the beginning routine.

BEGINNING ROUTINE

(MONDAY-WEDNESDAY-FRIDAY)

Exercise	Sets	Reps	% Men	% Women
Sit-Ups	1-2	20-30	—	—
Squats	3	10-15	40	25
Barbell Bent Rows	3	8-12	35	20
Upright Rows	2	8-12	30	20
Bench Presses	3	8-12	30	20
Standing Presses	2	8-12	25	15
Barbell Curls	2	8-12	25	15
Pulley Pushdowns	2	8-12	20	10
Standing Calf Raises	2-3	15-20	25	15

ADVANCED BEGINNING ROUTINE

(MONDAY-WEDNESDAY-FRIDAY)

Exercise	Sets	Reps
Bench Leg Raises	2	20-30
Seated Twisting	2	30-50
Leg Presses	3	10-15
Leg Curls	2	10-15
Seated Pulley Rows	3	8-12
Lat Machine Pulldowns	2	8-12
Bench Presses	3	6-10
Incline Presses	2	6-10
Upright Rows	2	8-12
Dumbbell Side Laterals	2	8-12
Alternate Dumbbell Curls	2	8-12
Lying Triceps Extensions	2	8-12
Barbell Wrist Curls	2	10-15
Calf Presses	3	10-15

INTERMEDIATE ROUTINE

(MONDAY-WEDNESDAY-FRIDAY)

Exercise	Sets	Reps
Sit-Ups	2-3	20-30
Seated Twisting	2-3	50
Squats	3-4	10-15

4

TRAINING WITH UNIVERSAL GYM EQUIPMENT

Universal Gym debuted their first exercise machine during the mid-1960s. It was originally touted for group use, particularly with athletic teams who could have up to 10 athletes training in circuit fashion at one time on a Universal machine. But gradually Universal machines gained favor throughout the weight training world because they offered the convenience of a variety of exercises performed on a single unit with easily adjusted weight stacks.

Universal Gym machines have been constantly upgraded with the addition of new exercise stations. And they have been manufactured for at least a decade with variable resistance features on some of the workout stations. An exercise becomes mechanically easier to complete as your arms or legs approach full extension, so Universal machines are constructed to apply an increasing amount of resistance toward the finish position of leg presses, bench presses, and shoulder presses.

The Universal machine at the original Gold's Gym in Venice, California, seems to be constantly in use, so we feel justified in saying that serious bodybuilders profit from using such equipment. Universal Gym units are best used as a supplement to workouts utilizing free weights and related equipment. But if you have available only a Universal Gym machine, you can still get in a fairly good workout using the exercises and routines presented in this chapter.

ADVANTAGES AND DISADVANTAGES

The primary advantage of Universal Gym units is their convenience. On a single machine, you can perform exercises for all parts of your body. And with a minimum of adjustment to the equipment, you can do any of twenty exercises for your own routine. You need only adjust the leg press seat position and select the amount of resistance you require for an exercise on the correct weight stack.

The main disadvantages of Universal equipment are cost and lack of variety in exercises. A Universal Gym costs at least five times as much as the price of the free-weight equipment required to stress comparable body parts. And only 3–5 exercises can be performed for each muscle group using Universal equipment, a factor which can lead to workout boredom. In contrast, you can perform at least 20, and as many as 50, movements for each muscle group using free weights.

SAFETY FACTORS

Universal machine training is inherently safer than working out with free weights, because it's impossible to be pinned under a heavy weight on the machine. However, there is one safety consideration that applies to Universal Gym workouts.

When you do heavy leg presses, be sure to keep your torso perfectly upright as you sit in the seat. Or, better yet, actually arch your back a bit as you perform the exercise. It's possible to strain your lower and/or upper back along the spine when doing maxed-out leg presses with your torso flexed forward, putting you in a hunched-back position.

EQUIPMENT ORIENTATION

Universal Gym was the first company to include on their equipment the popular adjustable weight stack used on virtually all exercise machines today. With such a weight stack, you can quickly and conveniently select a desired training poundage by removing the metal pin from the stack and replacing it at the appropriate level. Some weight stack pins must be rotated a quarter turn in order to remove them, then rotated a quarter turn in the opposite direction when you replace them, but you'll easily figure out how to work this type of pin.

The seat at the leg press station can be moved forward or backward by lifting a spring-loaded pin at the front of the seat, sliding the seat to a new position, and relocking the pin. Be sure that the seat is locked firmly in place before you use it, however, because a loose seat can give you an unexpected jolt if it slips to a new position in the middle of an exercise.

Most Universal Gym machines have two sets of leg press pedals, the lower set corresponding to the lower group of poundage figures on the weight stack and the upper set of pedals corresponding to the upper figures. Whenever possible, you should use the lower pair of pedals because they allow you to stress your quadriceps more directly than the upper pedals.

Functions of the various exercise stations of a Universal Gym unit will become obvious to you in the following illustrated exercise descriptions.

UNIVERSAL GYM EXERCISES

You will experience no difficulty in mastering the following 20 Universal Gym exercises because machine movements are much easier to learn than equivalent free-weight exercises. Simply compare the exercise descriptions with photos of the movement, then give the exercise a trial in your workouts.

LEG PRESSES

Stress points: Quadriceps, buttocks, hamstrings.
1. Adjust the seat position close enough to the pedals to force you to bend your legs to at least a 90-degree angle at the starting point of the movement. (The closer you position the seat to the pedals, the longer the range of movement your thigh muscles experience when doing leg presses; and the longer the range of movement of any exercise, the greater the benefit you receive from it.)
2. Sit in the seat with your torso erect and grasp the handles at the sides of your hips to keep your body in the seat as you do the exercise.

Leg Press, start.

3. Place your feet on the lower set of pedals attached to the lever arm of the machine, your toes pointed straight upward.
4. Slowly extend your legs to push the pedals as far from your hips as possible.
5. Return slowly to the point where the plates in the weight stack just touch each other, then repeat the movement for the required number of repetitions.

Leg Press, finish.

CALF PRESSES

Stress points: The gastrocnemius and related muscles at the backs of your lower legs.

1. Adjust the seat as far away from the pedals as possible.
2. Assume the same starting position as for leg presses, pushing the weight out until your legs are fully extended.
3. Keeping your legs straight throughout the movement, slide your heels from the pedals, until only your toes and the balls of your feet are in contact with the pedals.

Calf Press, start.

4. Allow the resistance attached to the lever arm of the machine to force your toes as far toward your head as is comfortably possible in order to stretch your calf muscles.
5. Extend your feet completely, pushing the pedals as far from your head as you can.
6. Slowly return to the position in which your calf muscles are fully stretched.
7. Repeat the movement for the suggested number of repetitions.

Calf Press, finish.

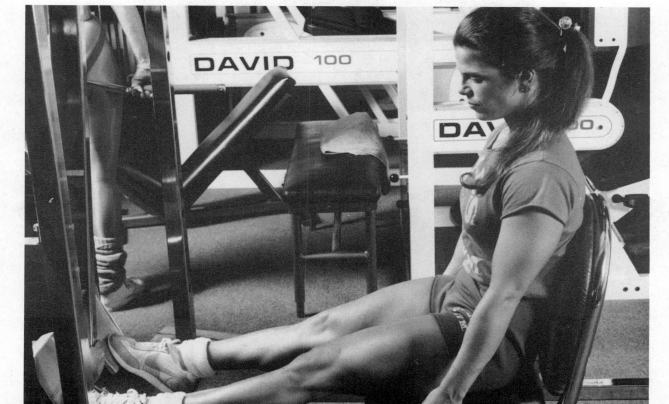

LEG EXTENSIONS

Stress points: The quadriceps muscles at the fronts of your thighs.
1. Sit at the end of the padded surface of the leg table toward the lever arm of the apparatus, your knees snugly against the edge of the table.
2. Hook your insteps beneath the lower set of roller pads attached to the lever arm.
3. Keep your torso upright during the movement and grasp the edges of the

Leg Extensions, start.

table to maintain your upper body and thighs in this position throughout your set.
4. Slowly straighten your legs completely.
5. Hold this peak contracted position for a moment, then slowly lower back to the starting point.
6. Repeat the movement for the desired number of reps.

Leg Extensions, finish.

LEG CURLS

Stress points: The biceps femoris muscles at the backs of your thighs.
   1. Lie facedown on the padded surface of the leg table, your knees at the edge of the bench toward the lever arm of the machine.
   2. Straighten your legs and hook your heels under the upper set of roller pads attached to the lever arm.
   3. Grasp the sides of the bench to keep your body steady as you do the movement, and be certain to keep your hips pressed firmly against the padded surface of the machine throughout your set.

Leg Curl, start.

Leg Curl, finish.

LAT MACHINE PULLDOWNS

Stress points: The latissimus dorsi, posterior deltoids, biceps, brachialis, and forearm flexor muscles.

1. Take an overgrip on the bar attached to the high pulley cable of the machine, your hands on the rubber grips (or near the ends of the bar, if there are no rubber grips).
2. Straighten your arms and either kneel or sit directly below the pulley.
3. Being sure to keep your elbows back, pull the bar directly downward to touch either your trapezius muscles at the back of your neck or your upper chest at the front of your neck.
4. Slowly return the bar to the starting point.
5. Repeat the movement for the recommended number of repetitions.

Universal Pulldown at midpoint.

SEATED PULLEY ROWS

Stress points: Latissimus dorsi, trapezius, erector spinae, posterior deltoids, biceps, brachialis, and forearm flexor muscles.

1. Attach either a bar handle or parallel-grip handle to the end of the cable running through the floor pulley of the machine.
2. Place two blocks of wood against the base of the machine for foot stops.
3. Grasp the handle, place your feet against the blocks, and sit down on the floor facing the pulley with your legs slightly bent.
4. Straighten your arms and lean forward in order to fully stretch your upper back muscles.
5. Simultaneously bring your torso erect and pull the handle in toward your torso, touching your hands or the handle to your upper abdomen.
6. Arch your back in the finish position of the movement.
7. Slowly return to the starting position.
8. Repeat the movement for an appropriate number of repetitions.

Seated Pulley Rows, start.

CHINS

Stress points: Latissimus dorsi, posterior deltoids, biceps, brachialis, and forearm flexor muscles.

1. Jump up and grasp the rubber grips on the ends of the chinning bar with your palms facing inward. (If the machine has a handle with right angles at each end, take an overgrip on the ends of the chinning bar.)
2. You can bend your legs at a 90-degree angle and/or cross your legs if you like during the movement.
3. Slowly pull your body up as high between the bars of the chinning station as you can manage.
4. Slowly lower yourself back to a position hanging at straight arms' length from the bars.
5. Repeat the movement for the stated number of reps.

Chins, behind neck, finish.

SHRUGS

Stress points: Trapezius and forearm flexor muscles.

1. Remove the bench from the bench press station.
2. Facing either toward the weight stack or away from the stack, take an overgrip on the handles of the lever arm and stand erect. (If you are short of stature, you might need to stand on a thick block of wood to be sure you are bearing the resistance attached to the lever arm in this position.)
3. Allow your shoulders to sag downward as far as is comfortably possible.
4. Shrug your shoulders upward as high as you can.
5. Slowly lower back to the starting point.
6. Repeat the movement for the correct number of repetitions.

Shrugs, start.

Shrugs, finish.

SEATED PRESSES

Stress points: Anterior/medial deltoids, triceps, and the upper back muscles that impart rotational force on the scapulae.

1. Place a stool between the handles of the shoulder press station of the machine.
2. Sit on the stool facing toward the weight stack, locking your legs around the uprights of the stool to secure your body in position. (Alternatively, you can face away from the weight stack as you do the movement.)
3. Take an overgrip on the handles attached to the lever arm of the station.
4. Slowly extend your arms to push the handles to straight arms' length overhead.
5. Slowly return your hands to the starting point.
6. Repeat the movement for the required number of repetitions.

Seated Press, start.

Seated Press, finish.

Seated Press, facing the machine, finish.

BENCH PRESSES

Stress points: Pectorals, anterior/medial deltoids, triceps, latissimus dorsi muscles.

1. Place a flat exercise bench between the handles attached to the lever arm at the bench pressing station.
2. Lie on your back on the bench, your head toward the weight stack and your feet placed solidly on the floor.

Bench Press, start.

3. Grasp the handles of the machine with an overgrip and rotate your elbows under your hands.
4. Slowly extend your arms and press the handles up to straight arms' length above your shoulders.
5. Slowly return the handles to the starting position.
6. Repeat the movement for the suggested number of repetitions.

Bench Press, finish.

INCLINE PRESSES

Stress points: The same as for bench presses, but with more stress on the upper pectorals.

Note: This movement is identical to bench presses, except that it is performed while lying back on a short incline bench.

Incline Press.

DECLINE PRESSES

Stress points: The same as for bench presses, but with more stress on the upper pectorals.

Note: This movement is identical to bench presses, except that it is performed while lying back on a decline bench.

Decline Press.

DIPS

Stress points: Pectorals (particularly the lower and outer aspects of the muscle group), anterior/medial deltoids, triceps.

1. Take a grip on the parallel bars in which your palms are facing inward, toward each other, when you are in the starting position of the movement.
2. Jump up to support your body on straight arms between the bars.

Dips, start.

Dips, finish.

3. Place your chin on your chest and flex your body slightly at the waist throughout the movement.
4. You can bend your legs at a 90-degree angle and/or cross your ankles during the movement if you like.
5. Slowly bend your arms and lower your body as far down between the bars as is comfortably possible.
6. Push yourself back up to the starting point.
7. Repeat the movement for the suggested number of repetitions.

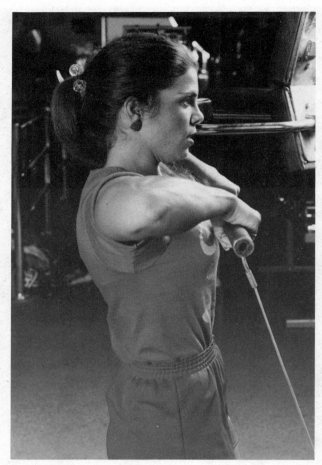

Upright Rows, finish.

UPRIGHT ROWS

Stress points: Deltoids (particularly the medial and posterior aspects of the muscle group), trapezius, biceps, and forearm flexor muscles.

1. Attach a short bar handle to the end of the cable running through the floor pulley of the machine.
2. Take an overgrip on the bar handle with your index fingers no more than 4–6 inches apart.
3. Stand erect with your feet set about shoulder-width apart 3-4 inches back from the pulley.
4. Extend your arms directly downward toward the pulley.
5. Moving only your arms and keeping your elbows above the level of your hands at all times, slowly pull the handle directly upward close to your body until your hands touch the underside of your chin.
6. Crunch your scapulae together in the top position of the movement.
7. Slowly lower the handle back to the starting point.
8. Repeat the movement for the desired number of reps.

PULLEY PUSHDOWNS

Stress points: The triceps (particularly the outer head of the triceps complex).
1. Attach a bar handle to the end of the cable running through the high pulley of the machine. (Alternatively, you can use a handle in which the ends are angled downward, or one consisting of two parallel strands of rope.)
2. Take an overgrip on the handle, your index fingers no more than 3–4 inches apart.
3. Stand erect with your feet about six inches back from the pulley.
4. Bend your arms fully and press your upper arms against the sides of your torso.
5. Keeping your upper arms and body motionless, slowly straighten your arms.
6. Return slowly back to the starting point.
7. Repeat the movement for the desired number of reps.

Pulley Pushdowns—start, left; finish, right. Note that upright in background is another machine, model Tom Platz is facing his machine.

CURLS

Stress points: Biceps, forearm flexors.

1. Attach a bar handle to the end of the cable running through the floor pulley of the machine.
2. Take a shoulder-width undergrip on the handle.
3. Set your feet a comfortable distance apart about 12 inches back from the pulley.
4. Stand erect and straighten your arms, pressing your upper arms against the sides of your torso.
5. Moving just your forearms, slowly bend your arms to curl the handle in a semicircular arc from the starting point to a position just beneath your chin.
6. Slowly lower back to the starting point.
7. Repeat the movement for the recommended number of repetitions.

Universal Curls, midpoint.

REVERSE CURLS

Stress points: Biceps, brachialis, and forearm supinator muscles.
Note: This movement is exactly the same as curls, except that it is performed with an overgrip on the bar.

Reverse Curls, midpoint.

WRIST CURLS

Stress points: Forearm flexors.

1. Attach a bar handle to the end of the cable running through the floor pulley.
2. Take a shoulder-width undergrip on the handle.
3. Sit down on a flat exercise bench about two feet back from the pulley.
4. Run your forearms down your thighs, your hands and wrists hanging off your knees.
5. Sag your fists downward as far as you can.
6. Use forearm strength to curl the handle upward in a small semicircular arc to a position in which your wrists are fully flexed.
7. Lower slowly back to the starting point.
8. Repeat the movement for an appropriate number of repetitions.

Wrist Curls, finish.

REVERSE WRIST CURLS

Stress points: Forearm extensors.

Note: This is precisely the same movement as wrist curls, except that it is performed with an overgrip on the handle.

Reverse Wrist Curls, finish.

HANGING FROG KICKS

Stress points: Rectus abdominis.
1. Adopt the same starting position as for chins.
2. Moving only your legs, pull your knees up to your chest while fully bending your legs.
3. Lower slowly back to the starting point.
4. Repeat the movement for the stated number of reps.

Hanging Frog Kicks, finish.

HANGING LEG RAISES

Stress points: Rectus abdominis.

1. Adopt the same starting position as for chins.
2. Bend your legs slightly and keep them bent like this throughout the movement.
3. Use abdominal strength to raise your feet in a semicircular arc to a point above the level of your hips.
4. Slowly return to the starting point.
5. Repeat the movement for the correct number of repetitions.

Hanging Leg Raises, finish.

UNIVERSAL GYM ROUTINES

If you are a beginner to progressive resistance training, you should perform the following Universal Gym routine on Mondays, Wednesdays, and Fridays.

Exercise	Sets	Reps	% Men	% Women
Hanging Frog Kicks	1-2	10-20	—	—
Leg Presses	3	10-15	100	70
Lat Machine Pulldowns	3	8-12	40	25
Bench Presses	3	8-12	40	20
Upright Rows	2	8-12	30	20
Seated Presses	2	8-12	30	15
Curls	2	8-12	30	15
Pulley Pushdowns	2	8-12	20	10
Calf Presses	2-3	15-20	80	50

(MONDAY-THURSDAY)

Exercise	Sets	Reps
Hanging Leg Raises	2-3	10-15
Leg Presses	3-4	10-15
Leg Extensions	2-3	10-15
Leg Curls	3	10-15
Chins	3	8-15
Lat Pulldowns	2	8-12
Shrugs	3	10-15
Seated Pulley Rows	2	8-12
Curls	3	8-12
Reverse Curls	2	8-12
Wrist Curls	3	10-15
Calf Presses	4-5	8-12

(TUESDAY-FRIDAY)

Exercise	Sets	Reps
Hanging Frog Kicks	2-3	15-25
Incline Presses	3-4	8-12
Decline Presses	2-3	8-12
Bench Presses	2-3	8-12
Seated Presses	3	6-10
Upright Rows	3	8-12
Pulley Pushdowns	3	8-12
Wrist Curls	2-3	10-15
Reverse Wrist Curls	2-3	10-15
Calf Presses	2-3	20-30

5
TRAINING WITH NAUTILUS EQUIPMENT

Nautilus inventor Arthur Jones tinkered with various exercise machines for a quarter of a century before finally unveiling his first Nautilus machines at the 1970 Mr. America competition in Culver City, California. At first Jones aimed his advertising campaign strictly at bodybuilders, primarily through ads in *Iron Man* magazine. But he soon turned to the more lucrative fitness and sports conditioning markets.

Within only a few years, Nautilus machines had become one of the brightest success stories in the bodybuilding/physical fitness industry, with yearly sales of more than $300 million. A majority of college and professional sports teams installed Nautilus machines to condition their athletes, and there are currently hundreds of Nautilus training facilities throughout the United States.

Within bodybuilding circles, Nautilus became reasonably popular among champion athletes, but certainly not as popular as free weights and related equipment. A few champion bodybuilders, such as **Mike Mentzer** (Mr. America) endorse Nautilus machines and training principles. They take short, highly intense workouts primarily on Nautilus machines and credit this type of training for their success in bodybuilding.

But a majority of bodybuilders consider Nautilus machines to be just another piece of training equipment that they can use to add variety or quality to their muscle-building workouts. They use machines individually in a workout for a selected body part, doing multiple sets of the Nautilus exercise rather than the single set recommended by Nautilus Sports Medical Industries. And they obviously have made great gains in muscle mass and quality exercising with a mix of Nautilus, Universal, and free weights.

ADVANTAGES OF NAUTILUS

Nautilus machines definitely supply a superior form of resistance in the exercises they allow a bodybuilder to perform. Nautilus exercises are of significantly higher intensity than movements performed with any other type of resistance training apparatus, due to certain advantageous biomechanical factors built into each machine.

Ellington Darden, Ph.D., in *The Nautilus Book* (Contemporary, third edition, 1985), enumerates the 10 elements of full-range exercise that are encompassed by Nautilus machines:

- Rotary resistance
- Positive work
- Negative work
- Stretching
- Prestretching
- Automatically variable resistance
- Balanced resistance
- Direct resistance
- Resistance in the position of full muscular contraction
- Unrestricted speed of movement

In comparison to free-weight exercises, Nautilus machines have an advantage in five of the ten forgoing elements. And Nautilus has this advantage because of the unique spiral pulley (called a "cam") that dictates the resistance placed on the muscle.

A Nautilus cam—as would even a perfectly circular pulley—provides resistance that is directly against the pull of the muscles at all times, as well as resistance in the fully contracted position of the working muscles. Both of these features are a result of the rotary resistance that is provided by a circular pulley or Nautilus cam.

The Nautilus cam, however, has features that cannot be found in a machine with a circular pulley. Due to the biomechanics of muscle contraction, a muscle can pull more strongly in some positions of an exercise than it can in others. And the Nautilus cams are designed to automatically accommodate this variation of strength in a muscle as it contracts over its full range of motion. A Nautilus cam automatically varies resistance in the correct parts of an exercise because of variations in the width of the cam. Where the cam is wide, it takes less strength to move the weight than where it is narrow. And the radius of each Nautilus cam is dictated by a computer that is geared to the natural strength curve of each working muscle group.

Above and beyond the biomechanical advantages of Nautilus training, Nautilus machines allow you to train in nearly total safety. Because the machines don't place stress on the working muscles in a resting position, you needn't worry about getting pinned beneath a heavy weight as you do a bench press or leg exercise. Nautilus and other types of exercise machines have the advantage over free weights and related equipment in this respect.

DISADVANTAGES OF NAUTILUS

Nautilus machines have two disadvantages, cost and lack of exercise variety. It would be prohibitively expensive to install a complete circuit of Nautilus machines in your home gym, and even a membership in a Nautilus facility is relatively expensive.

Only one or two movements can be performed on each Nautilus machine, and not more than four can be done for each part of your body using Nautilus equipment. As a result, experienced bodybuilders can grow bored training exclusively on Nautilus equipment. Many more exercises can be done for each body part using free weights and related equipment. This is the primary reason why experienced bodybuilders use a combination of free weights, Nautilus, and Universal—plus any other type of exercise machine available—in their muscle-building workouts.

CHOOSING A NAUTILUS GYM

At a pure Nautilus facility you will find long lines of machines arranged in the order that Nautilus Sports Medical Industries recommends their use. And in order to run the maximum possible number of facility members through the machine circuit, most facilities prohibit going through the machines in any order other than the way they are set up. And, members are not allowed to perform multiple sets on any of the machines.

Unless you can arrange a training time away from peak usage hours when the management allows you to use the machines in the order you would like to use them, and allows you to do multiple sets, you should avoid training at a gym that has only Nautilus machines. In that case, try to find either one that has some free weight equipment, or one that has some Nautilus machines to supplement their free-weight equipment. You will find that you get the best bodybuilding workouts when you can train with both Nautilus and free weights.

SAFETY FACTORS

Although safety factors are ignored in Nautilus literature, individual Nautilus facility managers have established two safety rules to be used when performing leg presses on a Nautilus leg machine:

1. Never hold your breath during the movement.
2. Never lock your legs out completely in the finish position of the exercise.

Since you will use maximum weights in your leg presses, these rules make good sense and should be observed.

NAUTILUS EQUIPMENT ORIENTATION

You shouldn't have any trouble performing the exercises explained in this chapter. As long as you follow the procedure outlined for each movement, you will do it correctly. However, you might have some difficultly in correctly adjusting the machine to fit your body.

In general, the center of the cams of the machine should be even with the main movement joint. If you are relatively short of stature, however, you won't be able to achieve this position without adding pads to the machine. These pads are usually available wherever you find Nautilus machines, and they can be placed under your seat or between your back and the machine backrest to bring your body into the correct alignment with the Nautilus cams.

Weights can be selected by moving a pin up or down the weight stack of each machine. But if you aren't able to make the full weight jump dictated by the weight stack, you can place smaller horseshoe-shaped weights on top of the weight stack to give you quarter- or half-plate jumps.

If you are a very strong bodybuilder, you will be able to do 8–10 reps easily with the full weight stack. In that case, you should set the pin at the bottom of the stack, then use a longer pin to attach a 25-, 50-, or 100-pound plate to the stack to add resistance to the movement. If you become strong enough to handle the biggest plate, you will need to add two or more plates to the basic weight stack to accommodate the strength of your muscles.

ADAPTING NAUTILUS FOR BODYBUILDING

If you read all of the books and other literature disseminated by Nautilus Sports Medical Industries, you will find that for bodybuilding purposes, you should train your full body three nonconsecutive days per week. You must also do only one set of each possible exercise in your routine, using maximum weights and forced reps or negative reps.

Very few champion bodybuilders or aspiring champs train strictly according to Nautilus exercise principles. In addition to avoiding Nautilus machines when training selected body parts, they usually do multiple sets of exercises performed on Nautilus equipment. And they may or may not include forced reps or negatives in their Nautilus sets.

The best way to describe how serious bodybuilders use Nautilus or Universal machines is to say that they *supplement* their free-weight workouts with selected machine exercises. Machines add variety to their workouts, which in turn maintains a high degree of workout enthusiasm and promotes faster gains from bodybuilding workouts.

We urge you to experiment with the type of workout just described, as well as with strict Nautilus workouts using Nautilus training principles. Then make up your own mind about which type of training is best for your unique needs as a bodybuilder.

NAUTILUS EXERCISES

In this section you will find 23 Nautilus exercises, each one fully described and illustrated so you can learn to perform it correctly without additional coaching. Some of these exercises are performed using obsolete Nautilus machines, but we include those movements because many gyms have the older types of machines rather than the new generation Nautilus equipment.

The first six movements are performed on the Nautilus multi machine, while the remaining movements must be done on individual Nautilus machines that can be found in a well-equipped bodybuilding gym.

CHINS

Stress points: Latissimus dorsi, biceps, posterior deltoids, brachialis, and forearm flexor muscles.

1. Stand up on the top step of a Nautilus multi machine.
2. Reach up and take an undergrip on the chinning bar, your hands set slightly wider than your shoulders on each side.
3. Straighten your arms and bend your legs to reach a position in which your body weight is supported by your hands beneath the bar.
4. You can bend your legs at 90-degree angles and/or cross your ankles if you like during the movement.
5. Use biceps and latissimus dorsi strength to pull your body upward until your chin is over the bar. If possible, actually pull your chest upward until it contacts the chinning bar.
6. Lower yourself slowly back to the starting point by extending your arms.
7. Repeat the movement for the required number of repetitions.

Chins, finish.

DIPS

Stress points: Pectorals (particularly the lower and outer aspects of the muscle group), deltoids (particularly the anterior aspect), triceps, and upper back muscles.

1. Stand up on top step of the machine and grasp the padded ends of the dipping bars with your palms facing each other.
2. Straighten your arms and lift your feet from the step to support your body at straight arms' length above the bars.
3. You can bend your legs at 90-degree angles and/or cross your ankles if you like.
4. Incline your head forward and rest your chin on your chest throughout the set.
5. Slowly bend your arms as fully as you can and lower your body as far as possible between the bars.
6. Slowly push your body back to the starting point of the exercise by extending your arms.
7. Repeat the movement for an appropriate number of repetitions.

Dips, finish.

DONKEY CALF RAISES

Stress points: The gastrocnemius and associated muscles of the lower legs.
1. Fit a hip belt around your waist just above your hip bones.
2. Step over to the multi machine, facing toward the lever arm.
3. Hook the hip belt to the end of the machine's lever arm.
4. Stand erect to bear the resistance of the weight stack and then step up to place your toes and the balls of your feet on the lower step of the machine.
5. With your legs held straight throughout the movement, bend over and rest your hands and/or forearms on the cross bar at the rear of the machine.
6. Allow your heels to travel as far below the level of your toes as possible to fully stretch your calves.
7. Rise up as high as you can on your toes.
8. Lower back down to the position with your calves fully stretched.
9. Repeat the movement for the desired number of repetitions.

Nautilus Donkey Calf Raise, midpoint.

SIDE BENDS

Stress points: The external/internal obliques at the sides of the waist.

1. Attach a loop handle or a loop of nylon webbing to the end of the lever arm of the machine.
2. Grasp the handle or loop of webbing in your left hand and stand with your left side toward the machine, your feet set a comfortable distance apart throughout the movement.
3. Keep your left arm straight during the movement and place your right hand either behind your head or on your hips as you do the exercise.
4. Keep your legs straight throughout your set.
5. Allow the resistance of the weight stack to pull your shoulders toward the lever arm, effectively bending your body at the waist to incline your torso toward the machine. Bend as far to the left as is comfortably possible.
6. Bend back as far to the right as you can.
7. Return to the position in which you are bent to the left.
8. Repeat the movement, bending to the right and then back again to the left for the correct number of reps.
9. Do the same number of repetitions with your right side toward the machine.

Side Bends—start, left; finish, right

WRIST CURLS/REVERSE WRIST CURLS

Stress points: Performed with your palms up, wrist curls stress the flexor muscles of your forearms; performed with your palms down, reverse wrist curls stress the extensor muscles of your forearms.

1. Attach a short bar handle to the end of the lever arm of a Nautilus multi machine.
2. Sit on a flat exercise bench or stool facing the lever arm of the machine.
3. With your palms either facing upward or downward, grasp the bar handle.
4. With your feet set about shoulder-width apart, run your forearms down

Wrist Curls, start.

Wrist Curls, finish.

your thighs so your wrists and hands are hanging off the ends of your knees.

5. Allow the resistance of the weight stack to pull your hands downward as far as possible.

6. Use forearm strength to curl the bar handle upward in a tight semicircular arc to as high a position as you can comfortably manage.

7. Return to the starting point and repeat the movement for the desired number of repetitions.

Reverse Wrist Curls, start.

Reverse Wrist Curls, finish.

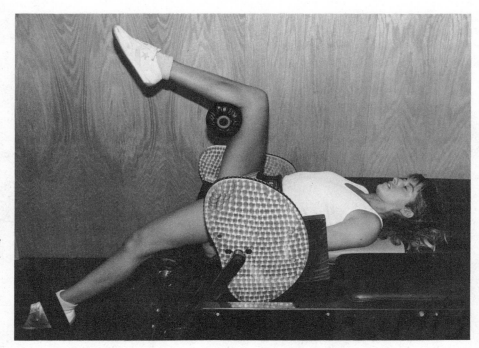

*Hip & Back machine
for right leg.*

HIP & BACK MACHINE

Stress points: Erector spinae, gluteus maximus, upper biceps femoris muscles.

 1. Lie on your back on the padded surface of the machine, your feet toward the lever arms.
 2. Drape your knees over the two roller pads and pull your hips toward the edge of the machine away from the weight stack until your hips are in line with the cams of the machine.
 3. Once you have your hips correctly oriented, fasten the lap belt firmly across your hips and grasp the handles provided at the sides of your hips to steady your upper body in position during the movement.
 4. Straighten your legs and push downward with them on the roller pads until your body forms one straight line (i.e., it is extended).
 5. Keep your left leg motionless and allow the right roller pad to slowly force your right knee as far toward your chest as is comfortably possible.
 6. Use hip and lower back strength to slowly force the right roller pad back to a position even with the left pad.
 7. Repeat the movement with your left leg, being sure to keep your right leg motionless.
 8. Do an appropriate number of repetitions with each leg to complete a set.
 9. When you are finished with your reps, allow both knees to move toward your chest until the lever arms stop.
10. Unbuckle the lap belt and exit the machine.

LEG EXTENSIONS

Stress points: Quadriceps.

1. You can adjust the back of some machines by lifting a lever on the right side of the machine and positioning the seat to the point where you can lean back against the seat with your buttocks against the seat back and the backs of your knees firmly against the edges of the seat toward the machine lever arm.
2. Sit in the seat and hook your toes and insteps beneath the two roller pads.
3. Secure the lap belt across your hips and grasp the handles at the sides of the machine to steady your upper body in position during the movement.
4. Lean back against the back rest of the seat as you do the exercise.
5. Slowly straighten your legs completely.
6. Hold this position for a count of two before slowly lowering the weight back to the starting point.
7. Repeat the movement for the suggested number of repetitions.

Leg Extensions, start.

Leg Extensions, finish.

LEG PRESSES

Stress points: Quadriceps, buttocks, hamstrings.
1. Adjust the seat of the machine forward so you cannot place your feet on the pedals at the end of the lever arm with your legs bent at less than a 90-degree angle.
2. Sit in the machine with your back against the back rest.
3. Buckle the lap belt over your hips and grasp the handles at the sides of the machine to steady your body in position as you do your set.

Leg Press, start.

4. Place your feet flat on the pedals in front of you, your toes pointed straight ahead.
5. Slowly extend your legs until they are just short of a straight position.
6. Bend your legs until the weight stack just contacts the plates not being used for the movement.
7. Slowly straighten your legs to return to the starting point.
8. Repeat the movement for the correct number of reps.

Leg Press, finish.

LEG CURLS

Stress points: Hamstrings.

1. Lie face down on the padded surface of the machine, your feet toward the lever arm of the machine.
2. Slide toward the lever arm of the machine and hook your heels under the roller pads. Your knees should be right at the edge of the padded surface of the machine once you have hooked your heels under the roller pads.
3. Grasp the handles at the sides of the machine to steady your body in position during the movement.
4. Press your hips against the padded surface of the machine and keep them in this position until you have completed your set.
5. Use hamstrings' strength to bend your legs as fully as is comfortably possible.
6. Hold this position for a count of two, then lower slowly back to the starting point.
7. Repeat the movement for the suggested number of repetitions.

Leg Curls, start.

Leg Curls, finish.

LEG ADDUCTION/ABDUCTION

Stress points: Adductions stress the thigh adductor muscles; abductions stress the hip abductor muscles.

1. Sit in the machine with your legs running down the movement arms of the machine.
2. By adjusting a lever at the right side of the machine, you can choose either the adduction or abduction mode of the exercise.
3. According to your choice, either force the lever arms toward each other or away from each other for the desired number of repetitions.

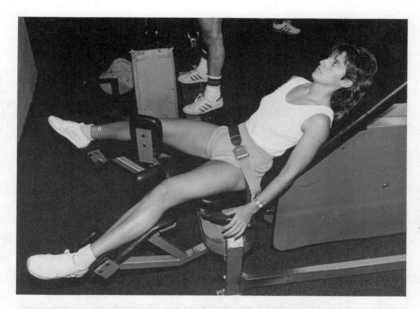

Leg Adduction.
Note position of pads.

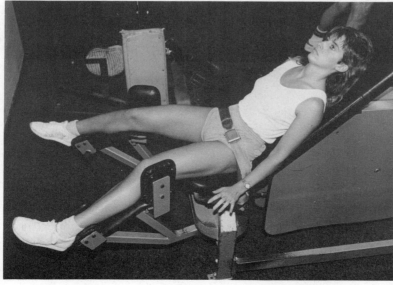

Leg Abduction.

CALF PRESSES

Stress points: The gastrocnemius and associated muscles of the lower legs.
1. Sit in a Nautilus leg press machine, place your feet on the pedals, and push with your legs until your legs are straight.
2. Once you have achieved the start/finish position for leg presses, slide your heels off the pedals until only your toes and the balls of your feet are in contact with them.
3. Keeping your legs straight, allow the weight of the machine to force your toes as far toward your face as is comfortably possible.

Calf Press, basic position.

4. Push with your toes and completely extend your feet.
5. Hold this extended position for a moment, then slowly return to the starting point.
6. Repeat the movement for an appropriate number of reps.
   Note: This is an excellent movement for building big calves, but it has been ignored in most Nautilus publications.

Calf Press, start.

Calf Press, finish.

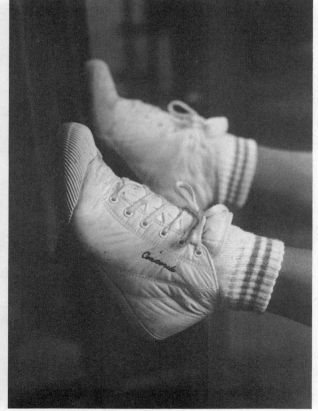

PULLOVERS

Stress points: The latissimus dorsi and other upper back muscles which place rotational force on your scapulae, pectorals, upper abdominals.

1. Adjust the height of the seat so your shoulders are at the same level as the cams when you sit in the seat.
2. Sit down in the seat and rest your back against the back support throughout the movement. Secure the lap belt.
3. Place your feet against the pedal directly in front of you and push down on the pedal to bring the lever arm of the machine forward to a position in front of your torso.
4. Place your elbows against the pads attached to the lever arm and lightly rest your fingers on the cross bar of the lever arm.

Pullovers, start.

5. Release foot pressure from the pedal to place full resistance on the lever arm.
6. Allow your elbows to travel in a semicircular arc as far to the rear as is comfortably possible.
7. Use the strength of your torso muscles to push the pads forward and downward in a semicircular arc until the cross bar attached to the lever arm contacts your abdomen.
8. Return slowly to the starting point.
9. Repeat the movement for the suggested number of repetitions.

Pullovers, finish.

Pulldown,
finish behind neck.

PULLDOWNS

Stress points: Latissimus dorsi and other upper back muscles which place rotational stress on your scapulae, posterior deltoids, biceps, brachialis, forearm flexor muscles.

1. Adjust the height of the machine's seat so it is at a level where you can just reach the handles of the lat bar when you are seated.
2. Sit down on the seat and secure the lap belt across your hips.
3. Reach up and take a grip on the ends of the handle so your palms are facing each other.
4. Lean slightly forward with your arms fully extended to stretch your upper back muscles.
5. Keeping your elbows back as far as possible, bend your arms to slowly pull the bar down to touch your trapezius muscles behind your neck. (Alternatively, you can pull the bar down to touch your upper chest in front of your neck.)
6. Hold this low position of the bar for a moment before slowly returning it to the starting point.
7. Repeat the movement for the suggested number of repetitions.

BEHIND NECK MACHINE

Stress points: This movement isolates stress on the latissimus dorsi and other upper back muscles that impart rotational stress to the scapulae.

1. Adjust the height of the machine's seat so your shoulders are even with the cams when you sit in the seat.
2. Sit in the seat and secure the lap belt around your hips.
3. With your palms facing forward, extend your arms directly upward and place your elbows against the inner edges of the roller pads.
4. Maintain your arms in a slightly bent position throughout the movement.
5. Use latissimus dorsi strength to push with your elbows against the pads, moving the pads outward and downward in semicircular arcs until the pads touch the sides of your torso.
6. Hold this fully contracted position for a moment, then slowly allow them to return to the starting position.
7. Repeat the movement for the required number of reps.

Behind Neck Machine, start, Behind Neck Machine, finish

SIDE LATERALS

Stress points: Medial/anterior deltoids and the trapezius muscles.

1. Adjust the height of the machine's seat to a level that puts your shoulder joints even with the machine cams when you sit in the seat.
2. Sit down on the seat, cross your ankles beneath the seat, and secure the lap belt across your hips.
3. Bend your arms at right angles and place your forearms against the inner sides of the pads attached to the machine's lever arms.

Side Laterals, start.

4. Being sure to move your elbows rather than merely your hands, use deltoid strength to move the pads upward as high as you can.
5. Hold this top point of the movement for a moment, then lower your arms slowly back to the starting point.
6. Repeat the movement for the recommended number of repetitions.

Side Laterals, finish.

SEATED PRESSES

Stress points: Anterior deltoids, triceps, and the upper back muscles that help to rotate the scapulae.

1. Adjust the height of the machine's seat the same as you would for side laterals.
2. Sit on the seat and secure the lap belt as for a set of side laterals.
3. Reach up and grasp the handles of the pressing slide with your palms facing inward toward each other.

Seated Press, start.

4. Extend your arms to slowly push the handles to straight arms' length above your head.
5. Hold this top point of the exercise for a moment, then lower the handles slowly back to the starting point.
6. Repeat the movement for an appropriate number of reps.

Seated Press, finish.

CHEST FLYES

Stress points: Lower/outer pectorals, anterior deltoids, serratus muscles.

1. Adjust the height of the machine's seat so your upper arms are approximately parallel with the floor when you are in the starting position of the movement.
2. Sit on the seat, secure the lap belt over your hips, and lie back against the angled pad of the machine.
3. Place your elbows against the pads attached to the lever arms of the machine, lightly grasping one set of handles with your hands.

Chest Flyes, start.

4. Allow the pads to travel as far to the rear as is comfortably possible to stretch your pectoral muscles.
5. Use pectoral strength to push with your elbows against the pads, moving them toward each other until they touch directly in front of your shoulders.
6. Hold the peak contracted position of the movement for a moment, then slowly return the pads to the starting point.
7. Repeat the movement for the stated number of reps.

Chest Flyes, finish.

DECLINE PRESSES

Stress points: Lower/outer pectorals, anterior deltoids, triceps.
1. Adjust the seat to the same height as for flyes.
2. Sit in the seat, secure the lap belt over your hips, and lie against the backrest.
3. Place your feet on the large pedal directly in front of your hips.
4. Push down on the pedal to bring the pressing handles forward enough so you can take a grip on them with your palms facing inward toward each other.

Decline Press, start.

5. Release foot pressure on the pedal to place weight on the pressing handles, allowing the weight to push your hands as far backward as is comfortably possible.
6. Slowly extend your arms to push the handles forward to straight arms' length in front of your shoulders.
7. Hold this finish position for a moment, then allow the weight to pull the pressing handles back to the starting point.
8. Repeat the movement for the correct number of repetitions.

Decline Press, finish.

BICEPS CURLS

Stress points: This movement isolates stress on the biceps with only minimal stress on your forearm flexor muscles.

1. Adjust the seat height to a level that allows you to run your arms upward along the pad in a direct line with your shoulder joints.
2. Run your upper arms along the pad, resting them against the small vertical pads throughout the movement.

Biceps Curl, start.

3. Grasp the handles attached to the lever arms of the machine with your palms facing upward and straighten your arms completely.
4. Use biceps strength to curl the handles simultaneously up to your shoulders.
5. Hold this peak-contracted position of the exercise for a moment, then lower the handles slowly back to the starting point.
6. Repeat the movement for the required number of repetitions.

Biceps Curl, finish.

TRICEPS EXTENSIONS

Stress points: This exercise isolates stress on the triceps muscles at the backs of the upper arms.
1. Adjust the height of the machine seat so you can run your arms comfortably up the pad.
2. With your fists toward each other at all times, place your fists and wrists against the pads attached to the lever arms of the machine.

Triceps Extensions, start.

3. Bend your arms fully, place your upper arms on the angled pad, and sit down on the machine seat.
4. Use triceps strength to completely extend your arms.
5. Hold this peak-contracted position for a moment, then allow the weight on the machine to push your hands back to the starting point.
6. Repeat the movement for the suggested number of repetitions.

Triceps Extensions, finish.

ABDOMINAL CRUNCH

Stress points: The entire rectus abdominis muscle wall.
1. Adjust the seat height so your shoulders are level with the pivot point of your shoulders.
2. Sit on the seat and wedge your toes and insteps under the roller pads. Your knees should be spread apart so your thighs run along each side of the raised portion of the seat pad.
3. Reach up behind you and grasp the handles of the machine, your palms toward each other.
4. Keep your back and the back of your head pressed against the padded surface of the machine throughout your set.
5. Use abdominal strength to move your shoulders toward your hips, exhaling as you contract your abdominals.
6. Hold this contracted position for a moment, then allow the resistance of the machine to pull you back to the starting point of the exercise.
7. Repeat the movement for the correct number of reps.

Abdominal Crunch.

ROWS

*Stress points:*1 This movement stresses the lats, traps, and other upper back muscles, plus the posterior deltoids.

1. Sit in the seat of the machine facing away from the weight stack.
2. With your palms facing toward the floor, force your arms between the roller pads so your elbows rest against the inner edges of the pads.
3. Keep your arms slightly bent throughout the movement, your palms toward the floor at all times.
4. Use upper back strength to push with your elbows against the roller pads, moving the pads backward in semicircular arcs as far as possible.
5. Hold the fully contracted position of the movement for a moment, then allow the weight to move the pads back to the starting position.
6. Repeat the movement for the desired number of repetitions.

Nautilus Row, start.

NAUTILUS BODYBUILDING ROUTINES

Here is a good, full-body, pure Nautilus routine that you can use on Mondays, Wednesdays, and Fridays:

Exercise	Sets	Reps
Abdominal Crunches	1	10-15
Hip & Back Machine	1	10-15
Leg Extensions	1	10-15
Leg Presses	1	10-15
Leg Curls	1	10-15
Pullovers	1	10-15
Pulldowns	1	10-15
Behind Neck Machine	1	10-15
Chest Flyes	1	10-15
Decline Presses	1	10-15
Dips	1	10-15
Side Laterals	1	10-15
Seated Presses	1	10-15
Biceps Curls	1	10-15
Triceps Extensions	1	10-15
Donkey Calf Raises	1	15-20

Note: Take every set to the point of momentary muscular failure.

Here is a more intense four-day split routine using only Nautilus equipment.

(MONDAY-THURSDAY)

Exercise	Sets	Reps
Abdominal Crunches	1	10-15
Side Bends	1	20-30
Hip & Back Machine	1	10-15
Leg Extensions	1	10-15
Leg Presses	1	10-15
Leg Curls	1	10-15
Leg Adductions	1	10-15
Leg Abductions	1	10-15
Chins	1	10-15
Pullovers	1	10-15
Pulldowns	1	10-15
Behind Neck Machine	1	10-15
Calf Presses	2	15-20
Wrist Curls	2	15-20

(TUESDAY-FRIDAY)

Exercise	Sets	Reps
Abdominal Crunches	1	20-30
Side Bends	1	30-50
Dips	1	10-15
Chest Flyes	2	10-15
Decline Presses	2	10-15
Side Laterals	2	10-15
Seated Presses	2	10-15
Biceps Curls	2	10-15
Triceps Extensions	2	10-15
Donkey Calf Raises	2	15-20
Reverse Wrist Curls	2	15-20

The Polaris 211 Total Triceps Machine.

6
ECLECTIC BODYBUILDING TRAINING

Our purpose in this chapter is to give you several intermediate-level bodybuilding routines for both your full body and individual muscle groups using free weights, Universal, Nautilus, and the wide variety of effective exercise machines manufactured by other companies. One might mistakenly conclude that health clubs are equipped only by Nautilus, Universal, and companies that sell barbells and dumbbells. But machines from Polaris, Maxicam, and other quality manufacturers are available in commercial workout establishments.

There are literally hundreds of exercise machines manufactured by companies other than the "Big Two"—Nautilus and Universal—available for use in gyms everywhere. Many of these machines are remarkably similar to apparatus manufactured by a different company, while many more machines are totally unique. We would be cheating you in this book if we didn't teach you how to combine these machines with other types of exercise equipment.

MANUFACTURERS AND DISTRIBUTORS

An extensive review of brochures, magazine advertisements, and books has given us a list of more than 50 companies that manufacture and/or distribute

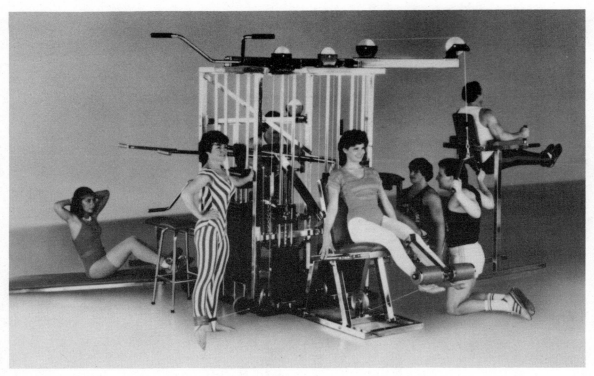

The FlexTech Centre.

resistance training equipment. In no particular order of quality preference, the following North American companies sell their own exercise machines: David Fitness Equipment, CamStart, Polaris, Bob Clark, Tom Platz, Power-max, Rocky Mountain Gym Equipment Company, Dax Fitness Industries, Weider Health & Fitness, Corbin-Pacific, Hercules, Dyna-Pack, Dynacam, Pro Star, Maxicam, Behnke Physical Fitness Equipment Company, TDS Barbell Corporation, Gross Industries, Buckeye Barbell, Body Masters Sports Industries, Ripped Gym Equipment, Vienna Health Products, Pitt Barbell & Health Food, Future Gym Equipment, Simisan, Queststar, Leo Stern, York Barbell Company, Body Exercise Equipment, Atlantic Fitness Products, Parabody, Soloflex, Smith, World Class, Pro-Gym Systems, Titan, Hunk Fitness Equipment, Fitness Industries, General Fitness Equipment, Hydra Gym, Paramount Fitness Equipment, Jubinville Exercise Equipment, Body Culture Gym Equipment, Keiser, and Zen-Tek Gym Equipment.

If we have left any manufacturer off this list, the omission was inadvertent. Keep in mind also that new companies will appear after this book has been published, and a few established firms will disband, so the list will be constantly changing.

You won't experience difficulty in learning how to do exercises on non-

Nautilus/non-Universal machines, because you'll be able to see other body-builders in the gym using them before you try one out. Additionally, there is quite an overlap of equipment design among the forgoing manufacturers. Just as one example, there are at least 20 brands of pec deck machines, each of which operates almost identically to all the others.

Despite the overlap of machine designs, however, each one of them will stress your muscles differently. And it's this great variety of machines that tend to develop the highest quality of physique.

ECLECTIC TRAINING

An eclectic bodybuilding routine is one that borrows from a number of sources, one that literally takes advantage of the best features inherent in every available type of resistance training apparatus. Eclectic training is advantageous because each exercise—even if it's similar to one done on another manufacturer's machine—places a unique stress on your working muscles. And the more different angles from which you stress an individual muscle group, the better will become its mass, strength, shape, and quality.

If you're a serious bodybuilder, don't make the common mistake of relying on only one type of resistance machine in your competitive workouts. Any experienced bodybuilder can instantly tell with a glance at your physique precisely which mode of training you have been using.

*Cindy Lefferts demonstrates the
Polaris 212 Lower Back Machine.*

Rick Stewart

The key to building a superior physique, whether you are a man or woman, is to train with heavy weights and low reps primarily on basic exercises, then alternate every workout between using free-weight movements and exercises on various machines with moderately heavy weights. This is the method used by many of the Mr. Olympias, Ms. Olympias, International Champions, and National Champions training at Gold's Gym.

In the balance of this chapter we will present proven and effective full-body training programs, then a bit later effective body part routines following the eclectic training philosophy.

ECLECTIC FULL-BODY ROUTINES

Four programs of progressively greater training intensity are presented in this section, moving up from a medium beginner's schedule to one suitable for a male or female bodybuilder just short of the advanced level of training.

For the record, the various machine names listed with suggested exercises were randomly chosen merely for the sake of illustration. If you don't have access to a machine recommended, simply use an equivalent apparatus. Every movement can be done with a wide variety of equipment to yield the same muscle-building results, and you should always feel free to choose your own mode of resistance.

Corbin-Pacific Bench Press

ROUTINE 1: BEGINNING LEVEL

(MONDAY-WEDNESDAY-FRIDAY)

Exercise	Sets	Reps
Sit-Ups	1-2	20-30
Universal Leg Presses	3	10-15
Nautilus Leg Curls	2	10-15
Seated Pulley Rows	3	8-12
Nautilus Behind Neck Machine	2	8-12
Universal Pulley Upright Rows	2	8-12
Nautilus Side Laterals	2	8-12
Polaris Seated Presses	2	6-10
Incline Barbell Presses	3	6-10
Body Masters Seated Bench Presses	3	6-10
CamStar Curl Machine	2	8-12
Nautilus Triceps Extensions	2	8-12
Barbell Wrist Curls	2	10-15
Calf Press (horizontal machine)	3	10-15

ROUTINE 2: ADVANCED-BEGINNING LEVEL

(MONDAY-WEDNESDAY-FRIDAY)

Exercise	Sets	Reps
Nautilus Abdominal Crunch	2	10-15
Corbin-Pacific Leg Extensions	3	10-15
Squats on Smith machine	4	10-15
Hercules Leg Curls	3	10-15
Body Masters Lower Back Machine	2-3	10-15
Polaris Behind Neck Machine	3	8-12
One-Arm Dumbbell Bent Rows	3	8-12
Nautilus Pullovers	2-3	10-15
Dumbbell Shrugs	1-2	10-15
Universal Incline Presses	4	6-10
David Pec Deck Flyes	3	8-12
Parallel Bar Dips	1-2	10-15
Nautilus Side Laterals	2	8-12
Nautilus Seated Presses	2-3	6-10
Cable Bent Laterals	2	8-12
Nautilus Biceps Curls	3	8-12
CamStar Triceps Extensions	3	8-12
Barbell Reverse Curls	2	8-12
Standing Barbell Wrist Curls	2-3	10-15
Seated Calf Raises	3-4	10-15

ROUTINE 3: LOW-INTERMEDIATE LEVEL

(MONDAY-THURSDAY)

Exercise	Sets	Reps
Hanging Leg Raises	2	10-15
Seated Twisting	2	50
Seated Leg Curl Machine	3	10-15
David Leg Extensions	3	10-15
Nautilus Leg Presses	4	20-10*
Nautilus Hip & Back Machine	2-3	8-12
Low-Incline Smith Machine Presses	4	12-6*
Body Masters Pec Deck Flyes	3	8-12
Wide-Grip Parallel Bar Dips	2-3	10-15
Dumbbell Wrist Curls	4	10-15
Seated Calf Raises	3	8-12
Calf Presses (vertical machine)	3	20-30

Note: Exercises marked with an asterisk should have weights and reps pyramidded each succeeding set.

(TUESDAY-FRIDAY)

Exercise	Sets	Reps
Incline Sit-Ups	2	20-30
Bench Leg Raises	2	20-30
Barbell Upright Rows	3	8-12
Chins Behind Neck	4	8-15
High Pulley Seated Rows	4	8-12
Polaris Lower Back Machine	2	10-15
Wide-Grip Barbell Curls	3	8-12
David Machine Curls	3	8-12
Close-Grip Bench Presses	3	8-12
David Machine Triceps Extensions	2	8-12
Universal Cable Reverse Curls	3	8-12
Standing Calf Raises	3-4	15-20

ROUTINE 4: INTERMEDIATE LEVEL

(MONDAY-THURSDAY)

Exercise	Sets	Reps
Body Masters Abdominal Machine	3	10-15
Nautilus Rotary Torso Machine	1-2	10-15
Universal Incline Presses	5	12-4*
Flat-Bench Dumbbell Flyes	3	8-12
Nautilus Decline Presses	3	6-10
Paramount Lateral Shoulder Machine	3	8-12
Seated Dumbbell Presses	3	6-10
Prone Incline Laterals Raises	3	8-12

Exercise	Sets	Reps
Dumbbell Upright Rows	3	8-12
Nautilus Pullovers	3	10-15
Front Lat Machine Pulldowns	3	8-12
Nautilus Behind Neck Machine	3	8-12
Barbell Bent Rows	3	8-12
Zottman Curls	3	8-12
Angled Calf Presses	3-4	15-20
One-Legged Calf Raises	3-4	10-15

(THURSDAY-FRIDAY)

Exercise	Sets	Reps
Wall Crunches	2-3	15-20
Roman Chair Sit-Ups	2-3	50
Nautilus Leg Extensions	4	10-15
Angled Leg Presses	5	15-6
Nautilus Leg Adductions	3	10-15
Corbin-Pacific Leg Curls	4	10-15
Jupinville Triceps Machine	4	8-12
Pulley Pushdowns	3	8-12
Barbell Preacher Curls	3	8-12
Corbin-Pacific Curls	3	8-12
Preacher Reverse Curls	2-3	8-12
Dumbbell Wrist Curls	3	10-15
Barbell Reverse Wrist Curls	3	10-15
Donkey Calf Raises (Nautilus version)	3	15-25
Standing Calf Raises	2	15-20

Routine 2 will be difficult to complete unless you are in excellent physical condition, because it includes such a large total number of sets. Therefore, the following two routines in this section will involve use of a split routine in which you train only part of your body each workout session, resting the fatigued muscle groups while you are bombing other body parts. All advanced bodybuilders use split routines, and if you wish to learn more about this advanced technique, please refer to its discussion on pages 100–01 in *The Gold's Gym Book of Bodybuilding* (Contemporary, 1983).

ECLECTIC BODY PART ROUTINES

In this section we will present one or two of each type of routine for all major muscle groups, one normal workout and one eclectic routine. And they are all of an intermediate-to-advanced level of intensity. For easy comparison, they are presented in parallel columns.

BICEPS ROUTINES

Conventional

Barbell Curls: 4 × 8-10
Incline Dumbbell Curls: 3 × 8-10
Dumbbell Concentration Curls: 3 × 10-12
Barbell Preacher Curls: 4 × 8-10
Wide-Grip Barbell Curls: 4 × 8-10
Barbell Concentration Curls: 3 × 10-15

Eclectic

David Curls: 4 × 8-10
Corbin-Pacific Curls: 3 × 8-10
One-Arm Nautilus Curls: 3 × 10-12
CamStar Curls: 4 × 8-10
Cable Curls: 4 × 8-10
Clark Machine Curls: 3 × 10-15

TRICEPS ROUTINES

Conventional

Pulley Pushdowns: 4 × 10-12
Erect Parallel Bar Dips: 4 × 8-10
Lying Barbell Extensions: 4 × 8-10

One-Arm Extensions: 4 × 8-12
Cable Pushaways: 4 × 8-12
Dips Between Benches: 4 × 10-15

Eclectic

CamStar Triceps: 4 × 10-12
Nautilus Extensions: 4 × 8-12
Dumbbell Kickback: 4 × 10-12

Nautilus Negative Dips: 4 × 12
Keiser Extensions: 4 × 8-12
Partner Towel Extensions: 3 × 10-15

FOREARM ROUTINES

Conventional

Barbell Reverse Curls: 4 × 8-10
Dumbbell Wrist Curls: 3 × 10-15
Barbell Reverse Wrist Curls: 3 × 10-15

Eclectic

Preacher Reverse Curls: 4 × 8-10
Wrist Rollers: 3-4 reps each way
Nautilus Allsport Twister

CHEST ROUTINES

Conventional

Incline Barbell Presses: 5 × 6-10
Parallel Bar Dips: 3 × 8-12
Flat-Bench Flyes: 3 × 8-12
Bench Presses: 4-5 × 6-10
Incline Dumbbell Presses: 3 × 8-12
Decline Dumbbell Flyes: 3 × 8-12

Eclectic

Nautilus 10-degree Chest: 3 × 12
David Pec Deck Flyes: 3 × 8-12
Decline Cable Flyes: 3 × 10-12
Nautilus Flyes: 3 × 8-12
Nautilus Decline Presses: 3 × 12
Jubinville Dips: 3 × 10-15

DELTOID ROUTINES

Conventional

Seated Barbell Presses: 4 × 6-10
Dumbbell Side Laterals: 3 × 8-12
Barbell Upright Rows: 3 × 8-12
Dumbbell Bent Laterals: 3 × 8-12

Dumbbell Upright Rows: 4 × 6-10
Seated Dumbbell Bent Laterals: 3 × 8-12
Seated Dumbbell Presses: 3 × 6-10
Front Barbell Raises: 3 × 8-12

Eclectic

Body Masters Press: 4 × 6-10
CamStar Side Laterals: 3 × 8-12
Cable Upright Rows: 3 × 8-12
Nautilus Rows: 3 × 8-12

Cable Upright Rows: 4 × 6-10
Standing Cable Bent Laterals: 3 × 8-12
Nautilus Side Laterals: 3 × 8-12
Cable Front Raises: 3 × 8-12

BACK ROUTINES

Conventional
Barbell Shrugs: 4 × 10-15
Front Chins: 4 × 10-15
Pulldowns Behind Neck: 4 × 10-15
Seated Pulley Rows: 4 × 8-12
Stiff-Legged Deadlifts: 3 × 10-15

Eclectic
Universal Gym Shrugs: 4 × 10-15
Nautilus Pullovers: 4 × 10-15
Polaris Behind Neck: 4 × 10-15
Floor Pulley One-Arm Row: 4 × 8-12
Nautilus Hip & Back: 3 × 10-15

ABDOMINAL ROUTINES

Conventional
Hanging Leg Raises: 3 × 15
Roman Chair Sit-Ups: 3 × 25
Bench Leg Raises: 3 × 20
Bench Crunches: 3 × 30
Seated Twisting: 3 × 50

Eclectic
Nautilus Crunches: 3 × 15
Nautilus Rotorary Torso: 3 × 20
Gravity Boot Crunches: 3 × max
Side Sit-Ups: 3 × 20
Abdominal Levers: 3 × 20

THIGH ROUTINES

Conventional
Leg Extension: 4 × 10-15
Squats: 4 × 10-15
Standing Leg Curls: 3 × 10-15
Lying Leg Curls: 3 × 10-15
Vertical Leg Press: 5 × 10-15

Eclectic
Nautilus Leg Extension: 3 × 10-15
Seated Leg Curl Machine: 3 × 8-12
Angled Leg Press: 4 × 10-15
Nautilus Leg Adductions: 2 × 15
Nautilus Leg Abductions: 2 × 15

CALF ROUTINES

Conventional
Seated Calf Raises: 3 × 15
Standing Calf Raises: 3 × 20
Calf Presses: 3 × 10
Donkey Calf Raises: 3 × 20
One-Legged Calf Raises: 3 × 15

Eclectic
Nautilus Donkey Calf Raises: 3-4 × 15
Nautilus Calf Presses: 4 × 15

CLOSING NOTE

With a little ingenuity, you can develop literally scores of routines for each muscle group using a combination of conventional and eclectic exercises. And the more different angles from which you stress a muscle group, the greater will be the ultimate quality of your physique. And that, amigos, is what bodybuilding is all about.

One of the best bodybuilding principles is what can be called the nonroutine routine. With this method—ideally suited to the type of training we've discussed in this chapter—you will never do the same training program twice. And this ultimate degree of variety in your training sessions builds muscle at an unprecedented rate of speed.

If you decide to give the nonroutine routine a trial, you should vary not only the exercises themselves, but also the angle of an exercise bench, the width of your grip on a barbell, the tempo of an actual set, the relative weight on the bar, and the number of repetitions performed in a set, either high, medium, or low. Just 3–4 weeks following such a program will convince you that it is incredibly effective.

7
BODYBUILDING DIET

Many young bodybuilders underestimate the importance of proper diet in the bodybuilding process. The general consensus of champions training at Gold's Gym is that diet accounts for approximately 50% of a bodybuilder's success formula during the off-season, with the other 50% accounted for by training.

Mike Christian says, "While diet and training go 50–50 in the off-season, the importance of diet rises as a competition approaches. I don't think it would be excessive to say that diet is at least 75% of the battle close to a competition. This is because a diet that is even mildly faulty will fail to strip away all the fatty deposits obscuring your muscles, leaving you looking smooth and unimpressive onstage. And in this type of condition, you will never win a major competition, regardless of how impressive your muscles are beneath the extra layer of fat."

Janice Ragain agrees with Mike: "But diet can be even more important for a woman bodybuilder than for her male counterpart because it's naturally more difficult for a woman to achieve a well-defined appearance to her physique. We have more body fat than men in relation to lean body mass, and our endocrinological makeup makes it even more difficult to lose this extra fat. A woman must maintain a faultless diet for a longer period of time than a man might in order to achieve true competition condition."

Beginning and intermediate bodybuilders will be in a constant off-season training mode, so you should think of your dietary program as 50% of your battle to the top in competitive bodybuilding. It will only be slightly more than 50% of the battle if you are initially overweight and must reduce your body fat percentage to maintain a normal appearance prior to entering a mass-building cycle.

LOSING WEIGHT

While a few bodybuilders follow low-carbohydrate diets, low-calorie regimens are more effective and promote a greater degree of overall health. If you need to lose body fat, you must reduce the number of calories consumed each day to a sufficiently low level to induce loss of fat. Since one pound of fat equals 3,500 calories, you must create a caloric deficit of about 500 calories per day to lose one pound of body fat in one week. It is both easy and safe to lose 1-2 pounds of body fat per week. And if you are careful to curtail the consumption of fatty foods and sugar-laden junk foods in your diet, you will experience little difficulty in consistently accumulating daily deficits of 500 calories or more.

When one gram of fat is metabolized in your body to produce energy, it yields approximately nine calories. In contrast, one gram of either protein or carbohydrate yields only about four calories, less than half as many as fat. So if you reduce your intake of fatty foods each day and replace the fats ounce for ounce with protein and carbohydrate foods, you will easily and naturally develop a caloric deficit. And doing nothing more than this will help you to reduce body fat stores without having to resort to constantly weighing and calculating the caloric content of each morsel of food you consume.

Those high-calorie foods that should be limited in your diet include beef, pork, ham, sausage, bacon, egg yolks, cooking and salad oils, butter, full fat milk and milk products, Brazil nuts (and most other nuts, excluding walnuts), artificial coffee creamers, coconut, chocolate, ice cream, most seeds (such as sunflower seeds), many grains (such as wheat), avocados, corn, bananas, and baked goods containing shortening.

These foods should be replaced by fish, chicken and turkey (with the fatty skin removed prior to baking or broiling), salads, melons, apples, strawberries, pineapples, celery, spinach, mushrooms, seed sprouts, cucumbers, tomatoes, squash, green peppers, rice, potatoes (but without butter or sour cream), and dry popcorn (without butter or salt).

A very interesting thing seems to happen to everyone who goes on this low-fat diet. For the first two or three days, you might find yourself constantly hungry. If you do, don't be afraid to eat all of the food you like, as long as it isn't a fatty food or an outright junk food containing refined sugar. Pig out on all of the watermelon and peaches you prefer or eat a lot of heavy bread, rice, or potatoes.

After two or three days of eating a healthy, albeit relatively high-calorie, diet, you will find that your body adapts to the new diet by naturally requiring less and less food each passing day. As long as you don't blow the diet by eating

Janice Ragain.

sugar-laden junk foods or fatty foods, you will soon find that your body has adapted to a relatively low caloric requirement. Then fatty pounds will melt off you, almost like a cube of butter melts in a hot skillet.

We know what you're probably thinking: "These guys are totally whacko, and there's no way this is going to happen." All we can ask is to just give it a try, and then make up your mind about how effective this low-fat/low-calorie regimen is in reducing body fat stores. You'll be surprised at how easy it is to reduce body fat stores on this simple, natural diet.

Following is a sample menu for one day of low-fat/low-calorie eating:

Breakfast: 3–4 egg whites scrambled with only one yolk, high-bran cereal with nonfat milk (but no sugar or honey to sweeten it), one piece of melon, herbal tea, supplements.

Lunch: tuna salad made with low-calorie dressing, dry baked potato, unbuttered slice of heavy bread, one or two pieces of fruit, iced tea, supplements.

Dinner: 1–2 broiled chicken breasts, rice, 1–2 green vegetables, salad with lemon juice, vinegar or low-calorie dressing, coffee, supplements.

Snacks: raw vegetables, fresh fruit, rice cakes, heavy bread, dry baked potatoes, nonfat yogurt.

You can feel free, of course, to modify this menu by deleting foods that don't appeal to you and including low-calorie dishes that you prefer to consume. Any diet can be individualized, as long as its caloric content isn't increased and you are able to maintain the diet for an extended period of time.

If you are initially overweight when commencing a bodybuilding program, you should remain on this diet until you have normalized your weight. Only then should you begin to follow the type of weight-gaining diet outlined in the following section.

GAINING WEIGHT

The news media lately has been big on exposing the huge numbers of obsese people in America, Canada, and the remainder of the world. Without question, there are millions of fatties out there. But equally without question, there are also millions of underweight individuals who would do almost anything to normalize their appearance. And these underweight men and women are seldom placed in the limelight by the news media.

In bodybuilding, we always talk about gaining muscular body weight rather than simply increasing weight by fattening up. Anyone can pork up simply by eating three or four pints of gourmet ice cream everyday in addition to a normal diet. And most men and women can gradually gain between 10 and 100 pounds of muscular weight by combining a sensible high-protein diet with moderately heavy weight training.

Muscle is built with the 22 amino acids consumed in a healthy, balanced diet. And the more protein consumed, digested, and made available in the bloodstream for assimilation into muscle tissue, the larger and stronger your muscles will become when they are regularly stressed by heavyweight workouts. Therefore, the main dietary objectives of a bodybuilder seeking to gain muscular body weight are to stay healthy and increase the amount of protein digested by the human stomach.

The protein-digesting capacity of your alimentary tract is limited to between 20 and 30 grams per meal, the exact amount determined by stomach size and relative digestive efficiency. So it stands to reason that you should eat frequent, high-protein meals to digest and assimilate a greater-than-normal amount of protein. And to promote digestive efficiency, these meals should be kept small and must consist of high-quality protein foods. (Heavy meals will actually tend to clog your digestive system and slow the digestive process.)

Human protein is made up, as we noted, of 22 amino acids. Of these 22, eight cannot be manufactured within your body and must be included in the food you consume. As a result, these eight amino acids are called *essential amino acids,* and a protein food that contains all eight essential aminos—plus most of the remaining 14—is called a *complete protein food.*

You should consume primarily complete protein foods in your frequent, small, daily meals. Complete protein foods almost invariably come from animal sources. Egg whites are considered to be the best source of bodybuilding protein, with milk, fish, poultry, and red meats also being important complete protein foods.

You can also take a protein supplement in the form of a blended drink in place of an occasional meal, as long as the protein powder comes from milk and egg sources. Protein shakes are particularly valuable when you are so rushed that you would ordinarily miss a regular meal. A protein drink can be prepared and consumed in a fraction of the time required for a normal meal. You will discover a basic recipe for protein drinks in the following section of this chapter.

Using the small, frequent meals plan-of-attack on an underweight condition, you might eat the following foods during one day of maintaining a weight-gain diet:

Meal 1 (8:00 A.M.): 4–6 eggs in an omelette with chopped ham and cheese, whole-grain toast with butter and/or honey, glass or two of milk, food supplements.

Meal 2 (11:00 A.M.): cold roast beef, a cup of flavored yogurt, raw nuts, milk, supplements.

Meal 3 (2:00 P.M.): protein drink.

Meal 4 (5:00 P.M.): steak, baked potato, 1–2 vegetable dishes, milk, supplements.

Meal 5 (8:00 P.M.): cold ham or hard cheese, hard boiled eggs, or raw nuts.

Meal 6 (11:00 P.M.): protein drink.

The final meal before retiring for the evening is essential to the weight-gaining process. Experience has shown us that a protein drink right before retiring gives your muscles plenty of protein with which to repair damaged tissues and increase muscle hypertrophy.

You will notice that milk plays a very important role in the weight-gaining process. This is primarily because milk is high in protein and calories and can be consumed quickly and easily to provide plenty of these key nutrients. Many of the biggest and most muscular bodybuilders of all time have been milk drinkers.

As good a food product as it is, however, milk still has drawbacks for those bodybuilders who are unable to efficiently digest it due to a lack of the enzyme *lactase* in their stomachs. This condition is known as *glactose intolerance,* and it's characterized by drowsiness soon after drinking milk, a bloated stomach, puffy tissues, and general malaise.

If you suffer from glactose intolerance, you can solve the problem by either taking lactase tablets or consuming more cheese and yogurt in place of the milk. You can purchase lactase tablets over the counter at most drug stores. Lactose, the component in milk that causes allergies, is removed from cheese and yogurt when milk is processed to form these foods.

FOOD SUPPLEMENTS

High-level bodybuilders make extensive use of concentrated food supplements, sometimes taking hundreds of dollars' worth of proteins, vitamins, and minerals each month when peaking for a major competition. If you decide to get serious about bodybuilding, you will ultimately spend many months— even years—experimenting with a broad spectrum of supplements to determine which individual food products best assist your bodybuilding efforts.

At the beginning and intermediate levels of bodybuilding, however, you should adopt a more fundamental and rational approach to food supplementation. We will explain only how to choose and use vitamin-mineral multipacks, vitamins B-complex and C, and protein supplements, the basic elements of a good bodybuilding nutritional program.

Before telling you how much of these four products to take, we would be remiss if we failed to explain where and how to purchase food supplements. First, you must learn to read food supplement container labels rather than making the common mistake of simply buying the most expensive product in each category. Hucksterism is rampant in the health food industry, so it's very common to see supplement distributors selling inferior products at wildly inflated prices. Even some of the biggest names in the industry will attempt to deceive you in this manner.

Read labels to determine the potency of each tablet or capsule of a vitamin or mineral product. Most companies list the potencies of vitamins and/or minerals for one tablet, but a common dodge of dishonest supplement promoters is to list the potency of 2–3 tablets or capsules. If you fail to recognize this fact when you read the label, an inferior product can be made to appear as if it had very high potencies of various vitamins and minerals. This misleading technique is most frequently used for expensive vitamins like B-complex and E, or for more costly amino acids like tryptophan, ornathine, and lysine.

Supplements can be purchased at health food stores and gyms, or via mail order ads inserted in various muscle mags. Gold's Gym, for example, sells a very good line of food products. But be sure to shop around and strive for the best values in each supplement. And *never* purchase a supplement merely because some champion bodybuilder endorses it!

Let's get to which supplements you need now and how much of each one

Samir Bannout.

you should take. We recommend taking 1–2 multipacks of vitamins, minerals, and trace elements per day, preferably with meals, as basic insurance against progress-halting nutritional deficiencies. Vitamin and mineral supplements should always be taken with meals, because these nutrients are most completely utilized in the presence of other foods.

In addition to a multipack or two, you can take vitamins B-complex and C individually, if doing so doesn't strain your budget too much. B-complex is a vital nutrient that helps you build new muscle tissue and stimulates your appetite. Vitamin C helps in tissue repair, fights infection, and heals injuries. Both of these vitamins are water-soluble, so it's impossible to overdose on them. Read the recommended dosage of each supplement on bottle labels and take twice the recommended amounts with meals, spacing the dosages out throughout the day.

The earlier section on weight-gaining introduced the idea of consuming protein drinks made from milk-and-egg protein powder. Milk and eggs are the best biological sources of protein, so a milk-and-egg protein powder will best complement your bodybuilding efforts. Avoid protein from vegetable sources, such as soybeans or yeast.

Using a milk-and-egg protein powder, here is a proven recipe for protein drinks:

- 8–10 oz. of whole milk
- 1–2 rounded tablespoons of protein powder
- 1–2 pieces of soft fruit for flavoring (e.g., strawberries, peaches, bananas, etc.)
- Shaved ice

Begin to mix the drink by pouring milk into a blender and then slowly sifting in protein powder with the blender set at a low speed. Increase blender speed to medium and add fruit. Add shaved ice and blend for 45–60 seconds at high speed with a top on the blender to yield a cold, frothy, delicious shake.

HEALTHY EATING

One main objective of bodybuilding nutrition is to consume foods that result in optimum health, because you will make your best bodybuilding gains only when you are healthy. Following are eight nutritional rules that, added to other information presented in this chapter, will help you to maintain optimum health.

- Don't use salted foods in your diet. Avoid highly seasoned foods. Don't drink artificially sweetened diet sodas.
- Avoid alcoholic beverages.
- Consume the widest possible variety of fresh, raw (or lightly cooked) foods.

- Drink at least 8–10 glasses of pure, fresh water each day.
- Prepare meals that are visually pleasing.
- Avoid junk foods, even when following a diet high in caloric content.
- Be consistent on any diet, because only a consistent dietary approach will yield the results you seek.
- Don't underestimate the value of proper diet in the bodybuilding process, because it is of supreme importance.

8
THE MIND IN BODYBUILDING

Champion bodybuilders feel that the mind is a key factor in making good gains in muscle mass. In terms of psychological approach, there is little difference between bodybuilders and successful athletes in any other sport. You will find numerous books on sports psychology in libraries and book stores. And you will read or listen to interviews of great basketball players, divers, and track athletes who extol the values of an optimum mental approach to their particular sport.

In bodybuilding, the acknowledged master of mental approach is Gold's Gym member **Tom Platz,** who has won the IFBB Mr. Universe title and placed as high as third in the Mr. Olympia competition. Tom observes, "The human mind is fantastically powerful. If you fail to maintain a correct mental approach to bodybuilding, you can actually train and eat optimally without making an iota of a gain in muscle mass or quality. The body always follows the course you set with your mind, so you must positively program your mind to achieve success in bodybuilding."

Don't wait until you start preparing for an upcoming competition before you kick in a good mental approach to the sport. You can and should begin using the mental techniques explained in this chapter at the beginning and intermediate levels of bodybuilding. You won't make fast gains until you *do* master these techniques.

TRACKING

Every time you encounter a new weight training exercise and begin to master it, you must build the correct nerve impulses between your mind and the muscles used to do the unfamiliar movement. And you will develop good neuro-muscular coordination for a new exercise more quickly and efficiently if you first mentally "track" the movement.

Tracking involves mentally picturing the exercise for a minute or two before moving through it with no weight, then with a light poundage, and finally with a full workout load. Tracking is also a first step to developing good training concentration, a mental skill that can't be mastered unless you have a picture in your mind of how each movement should appear and feel.

CONCENTRATION

Every successful bodybuilder can concentrate with great intensity on the working muscles in every set he or she performs in a workout. Concentration begins when you identify the muscle group(s) used to perform each exercise by using its exercise description, and the anatomy and kinesiology data in Chapter 2. It also begins with the mental picture and kinesthetic feel of the exercise developed as you track and physically learn the movement.

Next you must focus your attention on the main muscle group affected by the exercise (e.g., the pectorals when doing Bench Presses, even though the movement also stresses your deltoids and triceps). Many bodybuilders find that they can better feel the muscles strongly contracting when they do the exercise in front of a mirror and look at the muscles under tension. Of course, performing a movement in front of a mirror also allows you to visually monitor exercise biomechanics.

At first, you will find that you are easily distracted when you attempt to concentrate on a working muscle group. So, the trick to mastering pinpoint workout concentration is to immediately refocus your attenton on the stressed muscle group the instant your mind begins to wander. If you practice this process consistently, you should master total concentration on the working muscles for an entire set within a few short weeks, and for a complete workout within a few months.

At a serious bodybuilding gym you can easily detect the superior concentration abilities of elite athletes. Someone can speak to a good bodybuilder in the middle of a set without the athlete having heard a word due to his total concentration on the set being performed. And this is the level of training concentration you should seek.

POSITIVE THINKING

Invariably, champion bodybuilders maintain a consistently positive approach to life in general. More specifically, they have a positive approach to the entire bodybuilding process, including training, nutrition and mental approach.

It's unfortunate that modern society tends to condition developing boys and girls to accept a somewhat pessimistic view of life. Mom says, "Be sure that you don't get hurt when you ride your bike. A car could hit you." That's a negative statement. She doesn't often say a more positive, "Have an enoyable bike ride!" Don't get the idea that we are picking on mothers, however. We also receive negative conditioning from fathers, siblings, teachers, playmates, relatives, and many other sources.

Your immediate task is to begin thinking more positively. A glass should always be half full rather than half empty. You should think, "This exercise is going to do wonders for my arms." You should not think, "I wonder if this exercise will do anything for my arm development."

Once you are aware that you often think negative thoughts, it become easy to identify these counterproductive thoughts. And once you identify negative thoughts that spring unbidden into your mind, it becomes easy to replace them with positive thoughts.

Here's an example that will help you begin to change negative thoughts to positive ones. Most young bodybuilders end up thinking at some time in their involvement with the sport, "This exercise really hurts, so I should stop doing it before I injure myself." That sounds logical enough, doesn't it? But it's not logical at all.

Any experienced bodybuilder will tell you that a hard and productive set always hurts during the last couple of reps. But this isn't an injury pain, such as a sore joint. Instead, it's a deep burning sensation in the working muscles that's caused by a massive buildup of fatigue toxins in the muscles. Good bodybuilders actually seek fatigue-related pain, because they know it's a sure sign that they are benefitting from a set. So, it should come as no surprise that a favorite maxim of hard-driving bodybuilders is, "No pain, no gain."

The forgoing example is what **Rachel McLish** calls "turning the dial." And by this she means that there's a positive aspect to anything negative, and you can find this positive aspect if you look for it hard enough. So remember, the glass is *always* half full, *never* half empty.

GOAL-ORIENTED BODYBUILDING

One of the easiest high-level bodybuilding mental techniques to master is goal setting. Setting the right goals can make you a much more effective, efficient bodybuilder and shorten and smooth the long, hard road to your first physique title. Setting goals versus not setting goals is the same as the difference between firing a rifle at a target and randomly discharging it into the sky. Setting goals gives you a target at which you can shoot; setting goals gives you a well-ordered plan of attack.

You should set three types of goals: an ultimate goal, big long-term goals, and smaller short-term goals. If you read the profiles of elite bodybuilders in *Muscle & Fitness* magazine, you will find that virtually all top iron athletes have the same goal. Men wish to become Mr. Olympia and women want to become Ms. Olympia. These are the highest titles in the sport, so why not shoot for the moon?

It's fun to daydream about reaching an ultimate goal. And technically speaking, there's nothing wrong with aiming high, because setting your sights on the highest possible target allows you to shoot higher than you can under normal circumstances. But you must be realistic enough to realize that you may not reach your ultimate goal. After all, only eight men have won the Mr. Olympia title between its inception in 1965 and 1984; and only four women have been Miss Olympia between 1980 and 1984. One man and one woman win each year, and some bodybuilders, such as Arnold Schwarzenegger, are so dominant that they win these exalted titles repeatedly, excluding other potential winners from taking home the title.

Ultimate goals should be considered to be virtually impossible to reach. Think of them as a target that will motivate you to reach a higher point than you could reach on your own.

Long-term goals should be set yearly, and they *must* be realistically attainable. You can set several long-term goals each year. Since there is a direct relationship between lifting heavy weights and having a high degree of muscle mass, your long-term goals could be set in terms of exercise poundage. For example, a man can shoot for a 90-pound increase for Squats and a 60-pound increase for Bench Presses. Comparable feminine goals could be 45 and 30 pounds. And naturally powerful bodybuilders can realistically set poundage goals 50%–100% higher than these levels.

Many bodybuilders set yearly goals in terms of winning or placing high in competitions at increasingly lofty levels. **Lee Haney** (Mr. Olympia) followed this plan: "I took my career one step at a time. I first tried to win a state title, then a regional show, and later a national amateur title. Each step set me up to achieve the next level, and each new level achieved inspired me to shoot for the next highest level, until I won the Mr. Olympia title at age 25, becoming one of the youngest Mr. Olympias of all time."

Long-term goals should be subdivided into short-term goals that can be achieved at monthly intervals. And, much like Lee's step-by-step approach to winning big competitions, each short-term goal is an easy step toward reaching a tougher long-term goal. This process is sort of like eating a one-pound steak. You'd choke if you stuffed the entire steak into your mouth and tried to swallow it, but you can easily eat it one bite at a time.

Reverting back to the long-term poundage goals, you can divide them by a factor of 12 to arrive at short-term goals. If a long-term goal is to do Bench Presses with 60 additional pounds a year from now, you would reach this goal by achieving 12 short-term goals of five pounds each. And a five-pound goal is a hell of a lot easier to accept than a 60-pound goal.

Goal-oriented athletes develop a healthy type of tunnel vision. They develop a form of long-term concentration. And they become adept at developing an effective plan of attack on any problem, be it one in bodybuilding or any other theater of life.

Problem analysis skills come in handy. Whenever you are confronted with a big task, you will be able to quickly break it down to Step A, Step B, Step C, and so forth, until you have completed the task. No one puts a model ship together in one fell swoop. You have to glue Part A to Part B. Then you have to glue Assembly A-B to Part C. And a year later you have a model ship worthy of museum display.

PREWORKOUT PSYCHING

A few lucky bodybuilders seem to be mentally up for every workout. All they need to do is put one foot through the door of Gold's Gym, and they're so jazzed up for a workout that you couldn't hold them back with a Sherman tank.

The rest of the struggling masses of physique fanatics, including all four authors, have good days and bad days. Therefore, it would be advantageous if all of us strugglers had a foolproof way to get our unwilling minds and bodies just as jazzed for a workout as the lucky few.

The best preworkout psyching method we've enountered comes from hulking **Lou Ferrigno,** a member of Gold's Gym since 1976. Says Louie, "I save all of my old issues of various muscle magazines. I probably have close to 1,000 of them stored up, some are 30–40 years old. Whenever I don't feel up for a workout, I'll brew a cup of cappuccino and sit down to leaf through my collection. It usually takes about a half hour of this to work myself up for a workout.

"So, what psyches me up? It's just looking at photos of all the greats of years past, from Steve Reeves through Arnold Schwarzenegger and right up to Lee Haney. I'm one of them, so what am I doing wasting time when I could be in the gym pumping iron?! And I'm off to the gym for a super workout.

"Of course, you may not be a superstar bodybuilder yet, so your approach would be a little different when your peruse your old muscle mags. Maybe you can think, 'I have the potential to look like those bodybuilders, so I'll get into the gym and prove it.' And after you're psyched up, you will get into the gym and prove it!"

VISUALIZATION

The most effective mental technique used by all of the superstars of bodybuilding is visualization. You can read an advanced treatment of visualization in *The Gold's Gym Book of Bodybuilding,* but even at the beginning and intermediate levels of the sport, you can practice the visualization technique.

Visualization allows you to program your powerful subconscious mind—much as a technician can program a powerful computer—to assist you in your bodybuilding endeavors. And once your subconscious mind has been correctly programmed, you will be able to train hard more consistently, and more easily maintain a healthy, bodybuilding diet.

All in all, visualization is nothing more than creative, purposeful daydreaming. At a quiet time of the day—usually just before falling asleep, as long as you won't be interrupted—you will spend 15–20 minutes realistically imagining your physique the way you know it will soon appear.

Your visualized image should be as realistic as possible. It should include every new, striated ridge of hard muscle and all of the cuts between these ridges, cuts so deep and sharply delineated that you could hide a dime in one of them. It should include every spaghetti strand of blood-engorged vascularity. And it should include such miscellaneous features as the tight, satiny skin covering your musculature like a sheet of plastic freezer wrap; a deep tan (if you are initially fairskinned); and a degree of charisma almost oozing from your body as you run through a series of herculean poses.

Some bodybuilders fail to include faces, hair, hands, and feet in their visualized images, so be sure to make your image complete to the smallest detail. And once you get this purely visual (although visual in only an imagined context), you can move toward including the tactile sense of actually being inside that physique flexing your powerful new musculature, causing your muscles to bulge almost through your skin.

Psychologists have found that visualization involving all or most of your five senses will greatly improve the efficiency of program imprinting on your subconcious mind. So, you should endeavor to include the remaining three senses—smell, taste, and hearing. Smell can be as simple as the imagined scent of body oil as you pose, and hearing as simple as the roar of the audience as you surge powerfully through your posing routine. And taste can be the delicious taste of a foil packet of honey taken just before going onstage so energy is at a peak.

These are just samples of how you can include your five senses in a visualization experience. With imagination and accumulated experience, you will be able to easily come up with your own unique visualization situations.

Be sure to practice visualization every night if you can, and don't fear falling asleep with your image locked in your mind. Doing so will only imprint that image more indelibly on your subconscious mind.

You will find visualization to be a surprisingly pleasant experience, one you will look forward to repeating each evening. And with each visualization session, you will take a giant step toward achieving the fantastic new physique that you have visualized!

9
ONWARD AND UPWARD

The entire object of this book up to this point has been to instruct you in how to correctly learn each bodybuilding exercise you will encounter in your workouts, master the training techniques of a beginning–intermediate body-builder, and then get into the gym to actually take productive, muscle-building workouts.

But we've also attempted to interest you in the bodybuilding process as a whole, instilling in you the burning desire to build muscles that will stay with you for life. Some readers will become very interested in the bodybuilding process, some only moderately interested, and a few so disinterested that they bag the sport within a few short weeks.

The authors of *Solid Gold* have 50 total years of experience training young bodybuilders, so we can draw reliable conclusions about who will and who won't stick with the sport. It all boils down into thirds. About a third of all entry-level bodybuilders become so super-enthusiastic about the sport that they end up training and competing regularly, while another third ultimately wouldn't be caught dead in a weight room. The final third group of men and women—and we hope you at least fall into this category—stick with regular workouts and even monitor their diet to an extent, but they do so with less intensity than the competitive group of bodybuilders mentioned first.

Over a period of time you should gradually fall into one of these three categories. There's very little that we can do to encourage the group that never quite learns to love bodybuilding. Invariably they've had a gung ho physical education instructor or perhaps a Marine drill sergeant who turned them off of the pure joy of physical exercise. This is a shame, because virtually anyone who spends a month pumping iron will end up enjoying the activity, benefiting from even irregular weight workouts.

Those men and women who train for health, strength, and improved physical fitness invariably enjoy their workouts, and they enjoy the social atmosphere of a gym or spa. These bodybuilders are in a majority, and we would never try to change their approach to pumping iron.

The first group, the serious iron athletes desiring to develop a maximum degree of muscle mass, strength, and fitness—perhaps even peaking out for a bodybuilding competition—are the men and women we can most help in this chapter.

Knowledge is power in serious bodybuilding, and an aspiring competitive bodybuilder will quickly digest all of the knowledge we present in this book. So we will devote the balance of this chapter to a discussion of what additional bodybuilding knowledge you should seek out, and how you should go about evaluating the worth of each new piece of datum in relation to your own unique physique.

INSTINCTIVE TRAINING

Every man's and woman's body is unique. It responds somewhat similarly to all other bodies when subjected to external stimuli such as training and diet because there are firm laws of nature governing physiological processes within the body. But in myriad other ways, your body will respond to external stimuli differently from the way all other bodybuilders respond.

When you consider the hundreds of training and dietary variables that confront you, it would seem an impossible task to sort out the ones that optimally build your body. But once you master instinctive training ability, this task will be greatly simplified.

Instinctive training ability involves being able to detect and correctly interpret the biofeedback signals constantly being given to your body. Following are just a few of the biofeedback signals you should monitor:

- Muscle pump.
- Post-workout muscle soreness.
- Relative training drive.
- Ability to recuperate between workouts.
- Enthusiasm for workouts.
- Changing body composition.
- Hunger or lack of hunger.
- Sense of well-being.
- Increased workout poundages.
- Decreased rest intervals between heavy sets.

- Degree of workout concentration.
- Strength of the goal you're working toward.
- Change of muscle density (hardness).
- Greater prominence of muscularity.

You should be able to add at least 5–10 new biofeedback signals to this list once you've read the list and understand what types of signals you should be looking for. And the greater command you have of biofeedback, the more accurate your training instinct will be.

The more advanced you become as a bodybuilder, the more likely you will develop a "feel" for what is happening within your body. And this sixth sense develops as a result of monitoring the biofeedback data just enumerated and comparing it with how quickly you are progressing as a bodybuilder. When you develop this sixth sense, you have mastered instinctive training ability.

You become a scientist using your body as your laboratory when you have instinctive training ability. You can introduce one variable at a time into your experiment—low reps, high reps, forced reps, unique exercise combinations, differing lengths of recuperation between workouts—and determine how well each of the variables works to build muscle on your own unique physique. No one else can perform these experiments for you, because you are both the scientist and the laboratory.

With time and experimentation and observation, you will gradually eliminate from your philosophy ineffective and unproductive dietary variables, exercise techniques, and so forth. And in the end you will be left with only those training and dietary variables that will make you a winning bodybuilder without delay.

INFORMATION SOURCES

An integral part of the instinctive process of selecting techniques that work for your body is the availability of large bodies of written information about bodybuilding. At first you'll probably learn from talking with others in the gym where you work out, but information gleaned from other novice bodybuilders is usually incomplete and occasionally inaccurate. A far better source of information are the many books and magazines published about bodybuilding.

At the back of this book, you will find a bibliography that recommends key bodybuilding books and magazines that you should read to progressively increase your knowledge of the sport. These books and magazines are the most easily accessible sources of additional information on bodybuilding. And you have our assurance that only authoritative publications have been listed.

Another valuable written source of iron game information is the body of technical books and journal articles dealing with scientific aspects of bodybuilding, such as exercise physiology, biochemistry, anatomy, kinesiology, sports psychology and biomechanics. These scientific sources will be difficult to read at times, but they offer invaluable insights into the bodybuilding process.

A somewhat less valuable body of written material is the number of bodybuilding courses written by champion bodybuilders and sold via mail order ads in muscle mags. With only a few exceptions—the courses of Lou Ferrigno and Rachel McLish come immediately to mind—you won't learn anything in one of these pamphlets that hasn't already been published in magazine articles. So you would be better off spending your hard-earned bucks on back issues of the better bodybuilding journals.

In contrast to written material, personal contact with a champion body-builder can be invaluable. If you live near a Gold's Gym, you can meet the best bodybuilders in your area right on the gym floor. But be courteous enough to wait until they finish their workouts before you ask one of them a key question or two. Serious bodybuilding training demands intense mental concentration, which you could break if you pop a question in mid-set. And it's even possible for a champ to be injured if he's distracted in the middle of a very heavy set.

"If you don't live near a top bodybuilder," advises **Sue Ann McKean** (California Champion, Superbowl of Bodybuilding Champion), "you can still meet one at a seminar held by elite male and female bodybuilders throughout the country. These training and nutrition seminars are normally inexpensive, and they're advertised via posters in gyms in the area where the seminar will be held. You'll learn more than you might expect at one of these hands-on seminars, and a champion bodybuilder can give you intelligent answers to any questions that might have been bothering you."

Should you live in the backwoods of Alaska with the nearest bodybuilding seminar being held 3,000 miles away, you can still receive the advice of a champion. Many of these men and women answer training questions via cassette tapes. They list their services in *Muscle & Fitness* ads. It'll cost you more per piece of useful information via cassette than in a seminar, but the cassette method is readily available as long as you have a mailbox handy.

YOUR RESPONSIBILITY

Unless you live right next to Gold's Gym and have unlimited access to all of the superstars, you'll learn more about bodybuilding from reaching for the right books and magazines than from any other source. Reading will give you an excellent data base which you can refine once you do have access to champion bodybuilders who are willing to answer your more complicated questions.

As you can see from the bibliography at the back of the book, there are many bodybuilding magazines available on newsstands or through mail subscription. We know scores of aspiring bodybuilders who purchase every issue of each muscle magazine and accumulate hoards of back issues. As long as they read and reread all of the articles in these mags, we see no problem with the practice past a financial drain.

A better practice would be to purchase only the best four or five bodybuilding magazines each month. For both men and women, the best two are *Muscle & Fitness* and *Flex,* both published by Joe Weider. A couple of other excellent men's bodybuilding magazines are *MuscleMag International* and *Iron Man.* And the two best women's bodybuilding journals are *Women's Physique World* and *Strength Training for Beauty.* But keep in mind that bodybuilding magazines come and go, so this list may not be accurate by the time you read it.

As you gradually add to your bodybuilding library—and particularly when it is near completion—*use* it. Nothing is as worthless as a specialized collection of books that goes unread and unstudied. For at least a few minutes each afternoon or evening, you should sit down and continue reading a book that you started earlier. The more consistently you read your books and muscle mags, the more you'll learn about bodybuilding.

Reading is something like riding a horse. One day you might mount the horse and it will walk only a few steps before it refuses to budge any farther. Another time it may canter for a mile before stopping. But frequently the horse will decide to run at top speed for many hours. In reading terms, this is when you learn the most about bodybuilding.

What this discussion boils down to is the fact that an intelligent and educated bodybuilder has a big advantage over a lackadaisical man or woman who fails to study the sport. It shouldn't surprise you to learn that some of the most intelligent contemporary bodybuilders are big winners, like Arnold Schwarzenegger, Dr. Franco Columbu, Rachel McLish, Frank Zane, Lee Haney, and Corinna Everson.

We charge you to always seek new knowledge and better ways of doing things in bodybuilding. Never stop learning, because that's when you start to die in the sport. Instead, be a seeker, a learner, a winner!

James Gaubert.

GLOSSARY

AEROBIC EXERCISE—Long-lasting, low-intensity exercise that can be carried on within the body's ability to consume and process enough oxygen to support the activity. The word *aerobic* means literally *with air*. Typical aerobic exercise activities include running, swimming, and cycling. Aerobic exercise leads to cardiorespiratory fitness.

AFWB—The American Federation of Women Bodybuilders, the sports federation responsible for administering women's amateur bodybuilding in America. The AFWB is affiliated internationally with the IFBB.

AMDR—The Adult Minimum Daily Requirement for various nutrients, as established by the U.S. Food and Drug Administration.

ANAEROBIC EXERCISE—High-intensity exercise that exceeds the body's aerobic capacity and builds up an oxygen debt. Because of its high intensity, anaerobic exercise can be continued for only a short time. A typical anaerobic exercise would be full-speed sprinting on a track.

BALANCE—Referring to even body proportions, as in, "He has nice balance to his physique."

BAR—The iron or steel shaft that forms the handle of a barbell or dumbbell. Barbell bars vary in length from about four to seven feet, while dumbbell bars are 12–16 inches long. Bars are usually one inch in diameter, and they are often encased in a revolving sleeve.

BARBELL—This is the basic piece of equipment for weight training and bodybuilding. It consists of a bar, sleeve, collars, and plates. The weight of an adjustable barbell without plates averages five pounds per foot of bar length. The weight of this basic barbell unit must be considered when adding plates to the barbell to form a required training poundage. Barbells in large gyms are usually "fixed," with the plates welded or otherwise semipermanently fastened to the bars in a variety of poundages. These poundages are designated by numerals painted or engraved on the sides of the plates of each barbell.

BMR—The Basal Metabolic Rate, or the natural speed at which the body burns calories when at rest to provide its basic survival energy needs.

BODYBUILDING—A subdivision of the general category of weight training in which the main objective is to change the appearance of the human body via heavy weight training and applied nutrition. For most men and women bodybuilding consists merely of reducing a fleshy area or two and/or building up one or two thin body parts. In its purest form, bodybuilding for men and women is a competitive sport, both nationally and internationally, in amateur and professional categories.

BODYSCULPTING—This term is occasionally used in a feminine context to mean *bodybuilding*.

BURN—The feeling a muscle gets when it has really been pushed to its limits.

CHEATING—A method of swinging the weights or body to complete a rep that would have otherwise been impossible.

CIRCUIT TRAINING—A specialized form of weight training that develops body strength and aerobic endurance simultaneously. In circuit training a bodybuilder plans a circuit of 10–20 exercises covering all of the body's major muscle groups, then proceeds around the circuit in order while resting minimally between sets. Many bodybuilders use circuit training to improve their muscularity prior to a competition. As such, it is a good form of quality training.

CLEAN—The act of raising a barbell or dumbbell to shoulder height.

COLLAR—The cylindrical metal clamp used to hold plates in position on a barbell. Usually these collars are secured in place with a "set screw" threaded through the collar and tightened against the bar with a wrench. *Inside collars* keep plates from sliding inward and injuring a bodybuilder's hands, while *outside collars* keep the plates from sliding off the end of the bar. For safety's sake, you should never lift a barbell unless the collars are tightly fastened in place.

COUPLES' COMPETITION—Sometimes called "Mixed Pairs Competition," this is a new form of bodybuilding competition in which man–woman teams compete against each other. Couples' competition is becoming very popular with bodybuilding fans all over the world. It is now part of competitions even on the international level.

CUT UP—A term used to denote a well-defined bodybuilder. Usually this is a complimentary term, as in saying, "He's really cut up for this show!"

DEFINITION—This term is used to denote an absence of body fat in a bodybuilding competitor, so that every muscle is fully delineated. When a competitor has achieved ideal definition, his or her muscles will show striations, or individual fibers visible along a muscle mass. Definition is often called *muscularity.*

DENSITY—The hardness of muscle tissue, denoting complete muscularity, even to the point where fat within a muscle mass has been eliminated.

DUMBBELL—This is simply a shorter version of a barbell, which is intended for use in one hand, or more commonly with equally weighted dumbbells in each hand. All of the characteristics and terminology of a barbell are the same in a dumbbell.

EXERCISE—Used as a noun, this is the actual bodybuilding movement being done (e.g., a Bench Press or a Concentration Curl). An exercise is often called a *movement.* Used as a verb, *to exercise* is to work out physically and recreationally with weight training or any number of other forms of exercise (e.g., running, playing softball, etc.).

FLEXIBILITY—A suppleness of muscles and connective tissue that allows any man or woman to move his or her limbs and torso over a complete—or even exaggerated—range of motion.

FORCED REPS—A method of training whereby a training partner helps lift a weight just enough so the movement can be completed for two or three repetitions once the trainee has reached a point where he cannot complete it on his own.

HYPERTROPHY—The increase due to an overload on a muscle in that muscle's mass and strength. This is usually referred to by bodybuilders as *muscle growth,* though muscles do not grow in the sense of adding new cells to their mass.

IFBB—The International Federation of Bodybuilders, which was founded in 1946 by Ben and Joe Weider. It is the parent international federation overseeing worldwide, men's and women's amateur and professional bodybuilding. More than 115 national bodybuilding federations are affiliated with the IFBB, making bodybuilding the world's fifth most popular sport.

INTENSITY—The degree of difficulty built into weight training exercise. Intensity can be increased by adding resistance, increasing the number of repetitions done of an exercise, or decreasing the rest interval between sets. The greater the intensity of bodybuilding exercise placed on a muscle, the greater will be that muscle's rate of hypertrophy.

JUDGING ROUNDS—In the internationally accepted IFBB system of bodybuilding judging, three judging rounds are contested, plus a final posedown in which the top five contestants compete in a free-posing manner for added points. In Round I each bodybuilder is viewed standing relaxed with his or her front, left side, back, and right side toward the judging panel. Round II consists of a set of standardized "compulsory poses," while Round III is devoted to creative individual "free posing" to each contestant's own choice of music.

LIFTING BELT—A leather belt four to six inches wide at the back that is worn around the waist to protect a trainee's lower back and abdomen from injuries. The six-inch belt can be used in training, but only the four-inch belt can be used in actual weightlifting competition.

MASS—The size or fullness of muscles. Massiveness is highly prized in bodybuilding competition, especially by the male competitors.

MUSCULARITY—Another term for *definition,* it denotes an absence of body fat, so that every muscle is fully delineated.

NPC—The National Physique Committee, Inc., the sports federation responsible for administering men's amateur bodybuilding in America. Like the AFWB, the NPC is affiliated internationally with the IFBB.

NUTRITION—The various practices of taking food into the human body. Bodybuilders have made a science of nutrition by applying it either to add muscle mass or to totally strip fat from their bodies to achieve optimum muscle definition.

OLYMPIAN—An appellation given to those men and women who have competed in the Mr. Olympia or Ms. Olympia contests. Olympians are elite bodybuilders.

OLYMPIC BARBELL—A highly specialized and finely machined barbell used in weightlifting competition and heavy bodybuilding training. An Olympic barbell weighs 20 kilograms (slightly less than 45 pounds), and each of its collars weighs 2½ kilograms (5.5 pounds).

OLYMPIC LIFTING—A form of competitive weightlifting included in the Olympic Games program since the revival of the modern Olympics at Athens in 1896. Until 1972 this form of weightlifting consisted of three lifts: the Press, Snatch, and Clean and Jerk. Because of officiating difficulties, however, the Press was dropped from use following the 1972 Olympic Games, leaving the Snatch and Clean and Jerk as the two competitive Olympic lifts.

OVERLOAD—A degree of stress placed on the muscle that is over and above the amount the muscle is ordinarily used to handling. In bodybuilding this overload is applied by lifting heavier and heavier weights.

PEAK—Used two ways in bodybuilding jargon—to indicate the top of a muscle (usually the biceps) and to describe the process of reaching top physical condition before a contest.

PHA—An abbreviation for *peripheral heart action,* in which each skeletal muscle acts as an auxiliary heart by milking blood past one-way valves in the arterial system. Without PHA the heart itself would have difficulty circulating blood throughout the body. PHA is also a term assigned to a system of circuit training in which shorter series of four to six exercises are used in circuits. This system was pioneered by Bob Gajda, the 1966 Mr. America winner.

PLATES—The flat discs pierced with holes in the middle that are fitted on barbells and dumbbells to increase the weight of these apparatus. Plates are made of either cast metal or vinyl-covered concrete. They come in a wide range of graduated weights from as little as 1¼ pounds to more than 100 pounds each.

POUNDAGE—The actual weight of a barbell, dumbbell, or weight machine resistance used in an exercise.

POWERLIFTING—A form of competitive weightlifting using three lifts: the Squat, Bench Press, and Deadlift. The sport has both national and international competitions. Unlike in Olympic lifting, special women's competitions are held in powerlifting.

PROGRESSION—The act of gradually and steadily adding to the resistance used to overload a muscle group stressed by an exercise.

PROPORTION—A competitive bodybuilding term referring to the size relationships between various body parts. A contestant with good proportions will have no over- or underdeveloped muscle groups.

PUMP—To achieve a *pump* or to get *pumped* is to exercise a muscle until it is heavily engorged with blood.

QUALITY TRAINING—A type of workout in which the rest intervals between sets are drastically shortened prior to a competition. Quality training in combination with a low-calorie diet results in the best possible combination of muscle mass and muscle density.

REPETITION—Often abbreviated as *rep*, this is each individual full cycle of an exercise from the starting point of the movement to the midpoint and back again to the starting point. Usually, a series of several repetitions are done for each exercise.

RESISTANCE—As with poundage, this is the actual weight being used in an exercise.

REST INTERVAL—The pause between sets of an exercise during which the worked muscles are allowed to recuperate partially before the succeeding set is begun. Rest intervals vary from as little as 10–15 seconds to as much as five minutes. An average rest interval is about 60 seconds.

RIPPED—A term synonymous with *cut up*, as in "He's really ripped."

ROUTINE—Sometimes called a *program* or *schedule*, this is the complete accumulation of exercises, sets, and reps done in one training session. A routine is usually repeated two or three times each week.

SET—A distinct grouping of repetitions, followed by a brief rest interval and another set. Usually, several sets are done for each exercise in a training program.

SLEEVE—A hollow metal tube fitted over the bar of a barbell. The sleeve allows a bar to rotate more freely in your hands. Ordinarily, grooved knurlings are scored into the sleeve to aid in gripping the barbell when the hands have become sweaty during a training session.

SPOTTERS—Training partners who stand by as a safety factor to prevent you from being pinned under a heavy barbell during an exercise. Spotters are particularly necessary when you are doing limit Bench Presses and Squats.

STEROIDS—Prescription artificial male hormones that some bodybuilders use to increase muscle mass. Anabolic steroids are very dangerous drugs, however, and we do not recommend that anyone use them.

STICKING POINT—Any part of a movement that is very difficult to get past in order to complete the movement.

STRETCHING—A type of exercise program used to promote body flexibility. It involves assuming and then holding postures in which certain muscle groups and body joints are stretched.

STRIATIONS—This is the ultimate degree of muscle definition. When a muscle mass like the pectoral is fully defined, it will have myriad small individual grooves across it, almost as if a cat had repeatedly scratched the surface of a wax statue's pectoral muscles. These tiny muscular details are called striations.

SUPPLEMENTS—Concentrated vitamins, minerals, and proteins, usually in tablet/capsule or powder form. Food supplements are widely used by competitive bodybuilders, weightlifters, and other athletes to optimize their overall nutritional intake.

SYMMETRY—In competitive bodybuilding parlance, this is the shape or general outline of the body, as if it were seen in silhouette. Symmetry is enhanced in both male and female bodybuilders by a wide shoulder structure; a small waist–hip structure; small knees, ankles, and wrists; and large muscle volumes surrounding these small joints.

TRAINING TO FAILURE—Method of training whereby the trainee has continued a set to a point where it is impossible for him to complete another rep without assistance.

VASCULARITY—The appearance of surface veins and arteries in any bodybuilder who has achieved a low level of body fat. Women tend to have vascularity primarily in their arms, while male bodybuilders can have surface vascularity all over their bodies.

WEIGHT—Another term for *poundage* or *resistance*. Sometimes this term is used generally to refer to the apparatus (barbell, dumbbell, etc.) being used in an exercise, versus the exact poundage being used in an exercise.

WEIGHT CLASS—So that smaller athletes are not overwhelmed by larger ones, both competitive bodybuilding and weightlifting use weight classes. In women's bodybuilding the classes (at the time of this writing) were under 52½ kilograms (114 lbs.) and over 52½ kilos, while men's bodybuilding weight classes are set at 70 kilograms (154 pounds), 80 kilograms (176 pounds), 90 kilograms (198 pounds), and over 90 kilograms, or "unlimited." Powerlifting and Olympic lifting are contested in a much wider variety of weight classes. Converted to pounds from international metric equivalents, these are 114, 123, 132, 148, 165, 181, 198, 220, 242, 275, and over 275 pounds.

WEIGHTLIFTING—The subdivision of weight training in which men and women compete in weight classes both nationally and internationally to see who can lift the heaviest weights for single repetitions in prescribed exercises. Two types of weightlifting—Olympic lifting and powerlifting—are contested.

WEIGHT TRAINING—The various acts of using resistance training equipment either to exercise the body or for competitive purposes.

WORKOUT—A bodybuilding training session. "To work out" is to take a bodybuilding training session.

YOGA—An Eastern physical discipline that promotes body flexibility. Yoga also is a particularly tranquil philosophy of life.

BIBLIOGRAPHY

BOOKS

Aastrand, Per-Olaf, and Rohdahl, Kaare. *Text Book of Work Physiology.* New York: McGraw-Hill Book Co., 1977.

Bannout, Samir, with Reynolds, Bill. *Mr. Olympia's Muscle Mastery.* New York: New American Library, 1985.

Barrilleaux, Doris. *Forever Fit!* South Bend, IN: Icarus Publishing Co., 1984.

―――― and Murray, Jim. *Inside Weight Training for Women.* Chicago: Contemporary Books, Inc., 1978.

Bass, Clarence. *Ripped.* Albuquerque, NM: Ripped Enterprises, Inc., 1980.

――――. *Ripped 2.* Albuquerque, NM: Ripped Enterprises, Inc., 1982.

――――. *The Lean Advantage.* Albuquerque, NM: Ripped Enterprises, Inc., 1984.

Coe, Boyer, and Coe, Valerie, with Reynolds, Bill. *Boyer and Valerie Coe's Weight Training Book.* Chicago: Contemporary Books, Inc., 1982.

Coe, Boyer, with Summer, Bob. *Getting Strong, Looking Strong.* New York: Atheneum, 1979.

Columbu, Franco, Ph.D. *Franco Columbu's Complete Book of Bodybuilding.* Chicago: Contemporary Books, Inc., 1982.

――――. *Coming On Strong.* Chicago: Contemporary Books, Inc., 1978.

――――. *Winning Bodybuilding.* Chicago: Contemporary Books, Inc., 1977.

Combes, Laura, with Reynolds, Bill. *Winning Women's Bodybuilding.* Chicago: Contemporary Books, Inc., 1983.

Darden, Ellington. *High-Intensity Bodybuilding*. New York: Perigee Books, 1984.

———. *The Nautilus Advanced Bodybuilding Book*. New York: Fireside, 1984.

———. *The Nautilus Bodybuilding Book*. Chicago: Contemporary Books, Inc., 1982.

———. *The Nautilus Book* (third edition). Chicago: Contemporary Books, Inc., 1985.

———. *The Nautilus Nutrition Book*. Chicago: Contemporary Books, Inc., 1981.

Ferrigno, Lou, and Hall, Douglas Kent. *The Incredible Lou Ferrigno*. New York: Simon and Schuster, 1982.

Gaines, Charles, and Butler, George. *Pumping Iron*. New York: Simon and Schuster, 1974.

———. *Pumping Iron II: The Unprecedented Woman*. New York: Simon and Schuster, 1984.

Gironda, Vince, and Kennedy, Robert. *Unleashing the Wild Physique*. New York: Sterling Publishing Co., Inc., 1984.

Gray, Henry. *Anatomy, Descriptive and Surgical*. London: Crown Publishers, 1968.

Grymkowski, Peter, et al. *The Gold's Gym Training Encyclopedia*. Chicago: Contemporary Books, Inc., 1984.

Hatfield, Frederick C., Ph.D. *Bodybuilding: A Scientific Approach*. Chicago: Contemporary Books, Inc., 1984.

Kennedy, Robert. *Beef It!* New York: Sterling Publishing Co., Inc., 1984.

———. *Hardcore Bodybuilding*. New York: Sterling Publishing Co., Inc., 1982.

———. *Start Bodybuilding*. New York: Sterling Publishing Co., Inc., 1984.

——— and Mason, Vivian. *The Hardcore Bodybuilder's Source Book*. New York: Sterling Publishing Co., Inc.

Manion, Jim, with Manion, Denie. *Bodybuilding for Amateurs*. South Bend, IN: Icarus Publishing Co., 1985.

McLish, Rachel, with Reynolds, Bill. *Flex Appeal by Rachel*. New York: Warner Books, Inc., 1984.

Mentzer, Mike, and Friedberg, Ardy. *The Mentzer Method to Fitness*. New York: William Morrow and Company, Inc., 1980

———. *Mike Mentzer's Complete Weight Training Book*. New York: William Morrow and Company, Inc., 1982.

Murray, Jim. *Inside Bodybuilding*. Chicago: Contemporary Books, Inc., 1978.

Neve, Vickie. *Pat Neve's Bodybuilding Diet Book*. Phoenix, AZ: Phoenix Books, 1980.

Nutrition Almanac. New York: McGraw-Hill Book Co., 1982.

Pearl, Bill. *Keys to the Inner Universe*. Pasadena, CA: Physical Fitness Architects, 1979.

Platz, Tom, with Reynolds, Bill. *Pro-Style Bodybuilding*. New York: Sterling Publishing Co., Inc., 1985.

Reynolds, Bill. *Bodybuilding for Beginners*. Chicago: Contemporary Books, Inc., 1983.

————. *Complete Weight Training Book*. Mountain View, CA: Anderson-World, 1976.

———— and Vedral, Joyce L., Ph.D. *Supercut: Nutrition for the Ultimate Physique*. Chicago: Contemporary Books, Inc., 1985.

————. *Weight Training for Beginners*. Chicago: Contemporary Books, Inc., 1982.

Schwarzenegger, Arnold, with Dobbins, Bill. *Arnold's Bodybuilding for Men*. New York: Simon and Schuster, 1981.

————. *Arnold's Encyclopedia of Bodybuilding*. New York: Simon and Schuster, 1985.

———— with Hall, Douglas Kent. *Arnold's Bodyshaping for Women*. New York: Simon and Schuster, 1979.

————. *Arnold: The Education of a Bodybuilder*. New York: Simon and Schuster, 1977.

Sprague, Ken, and Reynolds, Bill. *The Gold's Gym Book of Bodybuilding*. Chicago: Contemporary Books, Inc., 1983.

Weider, Ben, and Kennedy, Robert. *Pumping Up*. New York: Sterling Publishing Co., Inc., 1985.

Weider, Joe. *Bodybuilding: The Weider Approach*. Chicago: Contemporary Books, Inc., 1981.

————. *Mr. Olympia*. New York; St. Martin's Press, 1983.

————. *The IFBB Album of Bodybuilding All-Stars*. New York: Hawthorne Books, Inc., 1981.

———— and Weider, Betty. *Body by Weider*. Chicago: Contemporary Books, Inc., 1984.

———— and Betty. *The Weider Book of Bodybuilding for Women*. Chicago: Contemporary Books, Inc., 1981.

———— with Reynolds, Bill. *Competitive Bodybuilding*. Chicago: Contemporary Books, Inc., 1984.

———— with Reynolds, Bill. *The Weider System of Bodybuilding*. Chicago: Contemporary Books, Inc., 1983.

Weider, Joe (Editor). *Bodybuilding and Conditioning for Women*. Chicago: Contemporary Books, Inc., 1983.

————. *Bodybuilding Nutrition and Training Programs*. Chicago: Contemporary Books, Inc., 1981.

————. *Building Arms for Mass and Power*. Chicago: Contemporary Books, Inc., 1983.

————. *Champion Bodybuilders' Training Strategies and Routines*. Chicago: Contemporary Books, Inc., 1982.

————. *Chest and Shoulders*. Chicago: Contemporary Books, Inc., 1984.

————. *More Bodybuilding Nutrition and Training Programs*. Chicago: Contemporary Books, Inc., 1982.

————. *More Training Tips and Routines*. Chicago: Contemporary Books, Inc., 1982.

————. *Nutrition and Training for Women Bodybuilders*. Chicago: Contemporary Books, Inc., 1984.

————. *The World's Leading Bodybuilders Answer Your Questions.* Chicago: Contemporary Books, Inc., 1981.

————. *Training Tips and Routines.* Chicago: Contemporary Books, Inc., 1981.

————. *Women's Weight Training and Bodybuilding Tips and Routines.* Chicago: Contemporary Books, Inc., 1982.

Wells, Katharine E., and Luttgens, Kathryn. *Kinesiology: Scientific Basis of Human Motion.* Philadephia: W. B. Sauders Co., 1976.

Zane, Frank, and Zane, Christine. *The Zane Way to a Beautiful Body.* New York: Simon and Schuster, 1979.

————. *Zane Nutrition.* New York: Simon and Schuster, 1985.

MAGAZINES

Bodybuilder, Charlton Publications, Charlton Building, Derby, CT 06418.

Flex, Weider Health and Fitness, 21100 Erwin St., Woodland Hills, CA 91367.

Iron Man, Box 10, Alliance, NE 69301.

Muscle & Fitness, Weider Health & Fitness, 21100 Erwin St., Woodland Hills, CA 91367.

MuscleMag International, Unit Two, 52 Bramsteele Rd., Brampton, ONT L6W 3M5, Canada.

Muscle Training Illustrated, 1665 Utica Ave., Brooklyn, NY 11234.

Muscle Up, Charlton Publications, Charlton Building, Derby, CT 06418.

Muscle World, Charlton Publications, Charlton Building, Derby, CT 06418.

Muscular Development, Box 1707, York, PA 17405.

Strength & Health, Box 1707, York, PA 17405.

FEDERATION ADDRESSES

International Federation of Bodybuilders, Ben Weider, International President, 2875 Bates Rd., Montreal, P.Q. H3S 1B7, Canada.

National Physique Committee, Inc. (Men), Jim Manion, President, 1050 Lafayette St., Bridgeville, PA 15017.

National Physique Committee, Inc. (Women), Candy Csencsits, Chairperson, Box 726, Lenhartsville, PA 19534.

INDEX